D1124672

THE ENTREPRENEUR'S GROWTH STARTUP HANDBOOK

Bloomberg Financial Series

Since 1996, Bloomberg Press has published books for financial professionals on investing, economics, and policy affecting investors. Titles are written by leading practitioners and authorities, and have been translated into more than 20 languages.

The Bloomberg Financial Series provides both core reference knowledge and actionable information for financial professionals. The books are written by experts familiar with the work flows, challenges, and demands of investment professionals who trade the markets, manage money, and analyze investments in their capacity of growing and protecting wealth, hedging risk, and generating revenue.

For a list of available titles, please visit our web site at www.wiley.com/go/bloombergpress.

THE ENTREPRENEUR'S GROWTH STARTUP HANDBOOK

7 Secrets to Venture Funding and Successful Growth

David N. Feldman

WILEY | Bloomberg PRESS

Library of Congress Cataloging-in-Publication Data:

ISBN 9781118445655 (Hardcover)
ISBN 9781118643051 (ePDF)
ISBN 9781118643273 (Mobi)
ISBN 9781118643297 (ePub)

Printed in the United States of America

10 9 8 7 6 5 4 3 2 1

To my amazing family, both actual, immediate, and extended.
Your support means everything and I love you all..

Contents

Acknowledgments

I am so thankful to so many who assisted me in this, my third book. Let us start with Bill Falloon and Meg Freeborn of John Wiley & Sons, the publisher of the Bloomberg Press imprint. Your patience and wonderful guidance were greatly appreciated. Thanks for the Hurricane Sandy extension when I lost power and Internet!

I am most appreciative to my entire family, but especially my 11-year-old son, Andrew, who encouraged me throughout the process, was interested in how the book came together, and as always brought comic relief to some of the moments. I want to thank Andrew for understanding when my writing time interfered with "man time" together. I promise we will make that up now and I love you so much!

As with my first book, allow me to re-recognize some who were early mentors. These include day camp impresario George Coleman, Carl Kaplan and Merrill Kraines at Fulbright & Jaworski; Gideon Cashman at Pryor Cashman LLP; and David Mazure of Smith Mazure. Of course, Uncle Lenny Rivkin (featured in Chapter 10) has been a lifelong mentor, advisor, friend, and father figure; and my cousin, his son, John, a good friend and advisor as well. Also thanks to former partners with whom I shared quite a few entrepreneurial lessons: Howie Griboff, Doug Ellenoff, Eric Weinstein, and Joe Smith.

Every entrepreneur is only as good as his most challenging employee. I want to say thanks to some folks who are or were with me for a long time. A tip of the hat to Stacey Spinelli, Melanie Figueroa, Adam Mimeles, and Jamie Bogart Shmuely.

I have enjoyed working with younger folks as my mentors did (and still do) with me. Most recently, thanks to Katie Shea and Susie Levitt for allowing me to mentor you and for showing me as much or more than I hope I have taught you. You're both got the stuff to be, and are, true entrepreneurs and, as they say, LYL. And to the various current and former clients and friends whose stories I have hopefully masked sufficiently to avoid identity, thanks for the experiences that brought me the little wisdom I bring to this effort.

To my newest colleagues at Richardson & Patel, in particular Nimish Patel, Erick Richardson, Kevin Friedmann, David Gordon, and Doug Gold, you are the best! Thanks for letting me concentrate on what I enjoy and think I do best: getting out to let the world know all about us, and managing complex transactions with the best team ever. To the rest of our fabulous R&P New York roster, including Melanie Figueroa (you get two shout-outs!), Gabby Napolitano, Melissa Solomon, Lukas Stuhlpfarer, Neal Wolkoff, Travis Meserve, Gus Smith, Elina Rozovskaya and Stella Zhao, you are all awesome; thanks for bringing us your talent and for your hard work.

I remain devoted to Youth Renewal Fund and its mission to help children, and offer special thanks to Sam Katz, Paul Schnell, and Karen Berman for their tireless efforts. To the team at Lawrence Woodmere Academy, thanks for seven great years of board service. I'm here if you need me!

Thanks to Bob Stein, David Smith, Kenny Lindenbaum, and my best man Eric Goodison for your fabulous personal advice over the years. And I am most appreciative for the friendship of Lucy Goetz, Jeff Meshel, Joe Lipton, Gregg Feinstein, Keith Lippert, David Bukzin, Gabrielle Guttman, Brittany Haas, and Richard Kendall.

To my mom, her terrific boyfriend, Fred Weinstein, my sister, Carol, and brother-in-law, Mike, and my late father, Dr. Ted Feldman, thanks for always being there for me. To my amazingly talented daughter, Sammi, nieces Lizzie and Tracey, and nephews Scott and Matthew, I'm very proud of and love you all.

I have been very lucky to have built my business network by making friends. To all of you, clients, contacts, and referral sources, you are the source of my success and my happiness. Thanks for helping me look forward to coming to work every day!

CHAPTER 1

Introduction

When I was about 8 years old, I decided to start saving money to buy baseball cards. The solution I devised: sell lemonade of course. My mom showed me how to make lemonade and I was in business. I set up my stand on the street near our home, put up a sign, and offered a paper cup of refreshing lemonade for five cents.

From my first sale, I was hooked. I loved the idea of business—selling things and making money from those efforts. In the winter, when lemonade didn't sell as well, I started shoveling snow to make money. From my early days as a "businessman," I found I had a bit of a knack for organizing things and seemed to draw people in as a leader. By sixth grade I was elected student council president, and on it went from there: editor-in-chief of my high school paper, head of my college radio station, and managing editor of my law school student newspaper.

My more serious entrepreneurial ventures started in college, when I became a partner in a children's day camp. In law school I bought a radio station. Later on I started and built my own law firms, managing them for 18 years. You will hear a bit about all of these in the pages ahead, along with tons of stories about my friends, clients, and contacts in my over 25 years of business and law practice.

My tiny childhood business was just the beginning for me. Do you have your own version of the lemonade story? If so, you may be the right type of person to start and build your own business. The hope is that this book helps you determine if indeed you have the right makeup for the travails of entrepreneurship, and how to navigate the biggest challenges one faces in creating and growing a business.

Why This Book?

Several years ago I wrote a series of columns for a small business web site maintained by Slate.com. With a little more negative outlook than here, the series was called "The Entrepreneur's Lament." It covered what I considered to be the seven things that a small business owner is likely to feel regret for or be upset about, and how to prevent these things from happening or fix them once they do.

I also wrote another series for the same web site called "Are You an Entrepreneur?" In this series I outlined what I considered to be the key personality characteristics most likely to lead to success in entrepreneurship. I based it on my years of working with hundreds of growing businesses and their founders, and of course from being one myself.

With this book we seek to combine and expand upon the content of these columns, adding many more real-life illustrative examples from my experiences. In some cases I have changed facts and names in order to protect my clients' confidential information. I think that anyone who is either thinking about starting a business, who has already done so, or who works with or advises entrepreneurs can benefit from the information provided here.

Even if you have run your own business for some time, there are helpful suggestions and areas of coverage that apply equally to those in the middle and more mature stages of building a business. For example, our discussion of boredom, burnout, and addressing a new exciting idea is more likely to affect entrepreneurs in later-stage situations.

There are a few themes to keep in mind as you are reading this. First, *entrepreneurship is not for everyone*. Just because you got laid off or are sick of your job does not mean you have what it takes to create and build something meaningful.

Second, *having the chops to be a great entrepreneur does nothing to guarantee that you will indeed succeed.* This book addresses only seven of the major challenges you will likely face. Accept the fact that many new businesses fail. It does not mean you weren't capable (though it might). As we will discuss, often it is things that are outside your control that cause a venture not to succeed.

Third, *remember that pretty much nothing goes according to plan all the time.* Much of this book is about how to deal with things that happen that you did not expect or get ready for. Indeed, hopefully a key message we are trying to convey is to have a plan, and make sure that plan includes things not following the plan.

There are many "how to" books out there on entrepreneurship, but none quite like this. Most talk about the mechanics of getting a business started and often tend to focus more on the basics of opening a small retail shop or one-person consulting business. Here we are more interested in those with big dreams and tremendous capability, experience, and drive who are ready to break out on their own, or already have.

Overview of the Book

This book has three key purposes. Chapter 2 asks whether you are indeed the right kind of person to build a successful business. Then Chapters 3–9, in no particular order, review a variety of issues that many will face in starting and growing something exciting in the entrepreneurial world. Many are challenges that, with careful attention, may be able to be avoided. If they cannot be avoided, hopefully they can be treated.

The final chapter, Chapter 10, pulls it all together. It focuses on the most likely reasons businesses fail, and some strategies for helping you avoid them. We then finish with a brief biography of a man who I believe embodies so much about what type of person should pursue his or her own business, and how he overcame much to build that success. Let's briefly summarize what the rest of the book provides.

In Chapter 2, we will provide an overview of the nine qualities that I believe dramatically increase the chance of being a successful entrepreneur. Briefly, these are: having the big dream, being a natural leader and decision maker, having an obsessive passion and drive, being a macromanager and a rational optimist, possessing a healthy fear of failure and little fear of risk, being controlling without being a control freak, and having a disciplined personal life.

Of course, as we will discuss, no one has all these qualities in abundance. The question is whether you have enough of them in sufficient quantity to improve your odds of success. Can a micromanager be a successful entrepreneur? The answer is "certainly." But I will posit that micromanagers may impede their ability to reach their business' full potential.

In addition to examples of those whom I have encountered with these qualities, we will spend a little time learning about folks ranging from Bill Gates to the Soup Nazi and even jailed former Enron chief executive officer Jeff Skilling.

Chapter 3 begins to delve into some of the challenges many entrepreneurs face. In this chapter we ask what you should do when a new great idea comes while you are still pursuing your original business. The answer is by no means simple. Something accretive to your business may indeed be a smart thing to work on, but it will take some of your focus away from the main original set of products or services you have been offering.

Sometimes the new idea is completely different from your existing business, yet seems exciting to you. This is certainly a tougher call to make. But whether the new opportunity fits or does not fit into your business, deciding *whether* to move forward is as difficult as deciding *how* to move forward if you are determined to do so. Chapter 3 will help you manage this process and provide some helpful tips.

In this chapter we begin talking about one of my business heroes, "shock jock" Howard Stern. He has built an extraordinary following for his radio show and related ventures. He has also avoided or treated many of the challenges we lay out in this book. We can learn much from Howard's success.

Chapter 4 addresses one of the great challenges that any entrepreneur faces: how to balance your work life with the rest of your life. This is indeed an age-old question for business owners, but must be addressed a little differently in the plugged-in, text-crazy world of today.

When you get total control of your business life and start a company, you can spend as much or as little time working as you want. So when it's up to you how do you do it? Can you ever really be "off"?

In this chapter we spend some time addressing the dreaded illness known as workaholism. We will learn the difference between being a hard worker and being "addicted" to work. We also introduce a running theme throughout the book, namely how these various issues affect female entrepreneurs differently from their male counterparts.

The chapter gives useful tips on finding ways to reduce your total hours by working smarter. We talk about getting you more time away not just for your enjoyment, but to actually enhance your focus and productivity. This includes not only family time, but also "me" time to do the things you enjoy on your own.

Chapters 5, 6, and 7 focus on important nuts and bolts aspects of building a business—getting the right employees, the right partners, and the right investors. These critical aspects of any business are particularly important for entrepreneurial companies. What can work for a large company often is unworkable for a small and fast-growing one.

Chapter 5 helps you determine what type of individuals are best to bring on as employees of your company. First we make clear that it is critically important to take the time necessary to hire the right people. Too many very busy entrepreneurs think, incorrectly, that their time is best spent elsewhere and employees are pretty much fungible.

The chapter then moves on to the process of actually finding folks who are a good fit for you. But it doesn't end there, as we then get into strategies for keeping employees motivated and satisfied. Sometimes an entrepreneur's ego doesn't make it easy to focus on keeping people that work for them happy.

We also explore the differences between hiring from large companies and "home growing" people you bring on at entry level or slightly above. Each has its challenges and benefits, as you might imagine. We urge you to look inward and be honest about the type of person you are in determining who the right employees are for you.

In Chapter 6 we handle the dicey issue of finding the right business partners. Much like finding the right person to marry, this is a critically important decision. In fact, you typically spend more time with your business partner than your spouse! That is, of course, unless your spouse is also your business partner, and we deal with a number of issues that can raise, along with more traditional family businesses.

Some realize that the best business partner is no business partner. We first examine whether going solo is for you. After all, for some the major draw of starting your own company is not to be answerable to anyone, including a partner. For others, there are many benefits to sharing the load.

If you do go the partner route, there are different issues depending on whether your new partner (or partners) founds the company with you, is a more passive investor partner, or is handed some equity either because he or she has made major revenue contributions to the company or is a critical "worker bee." We also review issues unique to partners who are best friends, romantic couples, or family members.

Chapter 7 brings us to an extremely important issue for an entrepreneur, namely the challenge of raising money for your company. In covering the six main methods of financing a growing business, we begin by looking at what drives the market for financing. In particular we review things that make the availability of funding more or less likely.

We then go through the basics of seeking capital, starting with how to make contact with sources of financing, then some specifics of the actual process of completing fundraising. From the initial meeting to disclosure documents and due diligence, the mechanics can be a little daunting for a first-timer.

The chapter then moves to a discussion of the six main methods of financing. These are bootstrapping, government financing, bank financing, "friends and family," angel, venture capital and private equity investors, and initial public offering or private investment in public equity (PIPE) financings for public companies.

Chapters 8 and 9 return us to some of the psychological challenges faced by entrepreneurs, namely burnout and boredom. These are very different issues but can be equally as challenging and debilitating.

In Chapter 8 we cover burnout. Some folks building businesses just reach a point of simple exhaustion. We begin with the causes of burnout, which can include family or spousal pressure, unexpected business pressures, and even surprising success that can wipe you out.

We then attempt to provide some advice for preventing burnout. Strategies include adjusting your plan when unexpected things happen, taking a break from things, and relying more on others to get things done. I say we "attempt," because this is advice that can be hard for many entrepreneurs to accept.

What to do when burnout hits comes next. Our suggested methods of dealing with it include selling or shutting down the business, or handing the business over to a colleague while you become a passive owner. Again, these are tough choices. For many their company is like a child. Do you want to sell your child? We work through these issues.

Chapter 9 turns to an often-underreported problem, primarily for really successful entrepreneurs: boredom. What could possibly be boring about running a successful, growing company? Boredom can be caused by too much growth, leading to a less "entrepreneurial" atmosphere within the company. It can also result from being, ironically, too successful in delegating the running of the business to other very capable folks. I have also seen boredom develop when a company founder, even though successful, finally realizes he or she entered the wrong business in the first place.

We then cover some ideas for preventing or overcoming ennui in business. As with burnout, you can sell or shut down the business. You can also hand the reins over to a top lieutenant and walk away continuing to own control of the equity.

The next suggestion is to check your personality when you start a business. If you hope and plan to build something substantial, are you the right kind of person to run the business when it reaches that level? We learn from greats who started on their own and stayed with their ultimately very large businesses happily like Steve Jobs, Donald Trump, Sanford Weill, and, yes, Howard Stern and Bill Gates again.

When boredom hits, another strategy is to re-engage in some aspect of the business that either is interesting to you or needs some attention. Instead of hitting Facebook for most of the day, sit and think about things you can improve in the business. We make a number of suggestions about methods by which to do this.

Chapter 10 finishes things up, trying to wrap up our discussion with a tidy entrepreneurial bow. We start with a discussion about what I consider to be the three most likely reasons an entrepreneur will not succeed: (1) lack of capital, (2) bad partner choices, and (3) personality traits that lead to burnout or loss of focus.

I then have the honor of completing our discussion with a brief biography of a very unique and special man I know who started with a one-person operation and built it to several hundred employees utilizing so many of the keys to success outlined here. I know you will enjoy "meeting" him in these pages.

Therefore . . .

Each chapter will conclude with a section called "Therefore . . . " that will ask the reader to think about the implications of what was covered and hopefully offer some useful advice as well.

I have enjoyed working with literally hundreds of excited entrepreneurs over the years. How many years? Your hint is that I reached a major milestone recently when I hired a new young lawyer who was born after I started practicing law. I have also been at times frustrated by watching smart people make the same mistakes as other smart people who came before them in my career. This led to the idea of the columns that led to the idea of this book.

So if you are ready, slide your finger across the e-reader screen (or you old-fashioned types go ahead and get a paper cut turning the page) and let's go!

CHAPTER 2

What Makes a Great Entrepreneur?

In my over 25 years of law practice I have represented many individuals who were starting or building their own business. In my case, after seven years working as an attorney in large law firms, I became one of them when I started my own firm. I continued running my own firms until 2010, when I combined my practice group with a larger firm, Richardson & Patel. I have also bought and sold several businesses along the way. So my perspective is unique in that I advise entrepreneurs but also personally have felt their pain through my own experiences.

I have often pondered what makes a great entrepreneur. Anyone can declare him or herself independent, leave their boring job and get that rush of excitement when they first de-shackle themselves from the corporate world. But even if they have the talent and ability in their industry, does that mean their makeup is such that they can handle the ups and downs, the stress, the dedication, and passion that are necessary to make a business succeed?

In particular in a time of a challenging economy, many laid-off or cut-back workers think seriously about starting something on their own. It is very tempting to be able to be your own boss, not answer to anyone, and let your own effort determine your compensation. But it is a simple fact that not everyone is cut out to do it.

This book focuses on just seven of the difficult challenges that most growth company founders face, but in the end—no surprise—we will conclude that despite all these burdens most entrepreneurs would not trade what they are doing. So, do you have what it takes?

There are tens of millions of responses when you ask Google "Are you an entrepreneur?" I looked it up *after* creating my list, and was surprised. First by how many online answers were similar to my list, second by how many of the online answers I strongly disagree with, and last the number that I came up with that simply did not seem to appear anywhere online. In this analysis, we are not talking about the businesspeople with fleeting thoughts of opening a Subway franchise someday. I am talking about people with a desire to build something substantial and significant. I also assume that you have the savvy and experience in your industry to break out on your own.

In my career I have watched and worked with entrepreneurs in industries as diverse as healthcare, mining, biotechnology, accounting, law, finance and investment banking, software and technology, business equipment, consumer products, telecommunications, Internet businesses, and more. I have worked with companies all over the world, from the United States to the UK to Hungary to China, Brazil, Israel, and Italy.

Amazingly, though, much is the same across industries and geography as to what it takes to build a successful business, and I believe there are nine key personality traits that dramatically increase your chances of being a successful entrepreneur. They are: big dreamer, natural leader and decision maker, obsessive passion and drive, macromanager, rational optimist, healthy fear of failure, little fear of risk, controlling but not freakish, and disciplined personal and business life.

For you speed readers, let's start with a quick sentence or two on each.

- *Big dreamer.* You look at the way Microsoft and Home Depot started very small and believe you can do the same thing. You have, as my wife likes to say, that million-dollar idea.
- *Natural leader and decision maker.* You are a great communicator and good listener; people trust and follow you. You relish the opportunity to efficiently weigh important choices, then roll the dice and monitor implementation.
- *Obsessive passion and drive.* It is not possible to be a successful entrepreneur without a major appetite to dive into what you are doing. You pop out of bed each morning excited for the day ahead. The clock is less important than completing your goals for the day, and you simply will not rest until you are satisfied.
- *Macromanager.* I learned that I did not coin this phrase, but it is obviously the opposite of being a micromanager. The best entrepreneurs learn to delegate day-to-day tasks, leaving them to the important business of dreaming, planning, assisting with key hires, and helping solve the major problems that arise.
- *Rational optimist.* I admit that at times I fail on this one, at least the rational part. The best entrepreneurs plow ahead thinking the best is right around the corner, but attempt to quell that enthusiasm with preparation for difficulties ahead.

- *Healthy fear of failure.* This follows directly from rational optimism. Part of what drives me every day is the ringing in my head of "When are they going to take this all away?"
- *Little fear of risk.* Entrepreneurs understand that the greatest rewards await those who risk the most.
- *Controlling but not freakish.* A true control freak will not make a great entrepreneur. But healthy skepticism of the talents and motivations of those around you is not a bad thing. However, if you are not careful this conflicts with trying to be a successful macromanager.
- *Disciplined personal and business life.* Many entrepreneurs' guides talk about the importance of being healthy. Yes, that's important, but it's best overall to lead a fully disciplined life. The risk-taking mentality also has a dark side, as it too often goes together with other, less-favorable, risky behavior.

So let's take these traits on one at a time.

The Big Dream

We start with what may be the single most important characteristic of great business impresarios: being a big dreamer. I always think of the classic 1950s TV show *The Honeymooners*. Always downtrodden New York City bus driver Ralph Kramden (played by comic legend Jackie Gleason) kept looking for that one idea or project that would take him and his wife, Alice, to easy street. "This is the big one, honey," he would scream. Of course each time his hopes were dashed, but he realized what really mattered in his life were good friend Norton and his great wife, Alice.

Great entrepreneurs have that same excitement, though hopefully with better success than poor Ralph. The key is figuring out something you can do differently or better than everything else out there. Or find something that's never been done. Note that simple technological or other advance, by itself, is only the beginning. Someone has to know how to take that advance to the market, and it has to satisfy some unmet need that exists. Some of us of a certain age remember great advances like the Sony Betamax video recorder and Quadrophonic stereo that bombed ultimately.

But there are other great ideas, even though maybe not as dramatic as a true breakthrough. For example, I started my own law firms doing something that I believe was unique. I centered the strategy on basic marketing concepts. I asked myself, what are the two things that clients complain about the most when dissatisfied with their lawyer? If you assume the lawyer is competent, the two main things are: He or she charges too much, and he or she doesn't get back to me quickly enough. You can be a great lawyer, but if you overcharge or are inaccessible, you are basically worthless to the client.

In dealing with these, I immediately established an absolute four-hour telephone callback rule for clients. When they call any lawyer in our shop, they will for sure receive a call back within four business hours. Of course, in most cases response time is even shorter. Any firm would say they do the same, but not all actually do it. And none, that I know of, make it formal policy. Differentiation.

In the area of fees, while I did not invent flat fees, we embraced them for corporate transactional work almost 20 years ago, when it was quite controversial indeed. I believe billing by the hour is a conflict of interest between me and my client, and even when you bill honorably, many clients still suspect that you are not. The flat fee removes that concern. It also helps bring a wary potential client through the threshold by eliminating one major uncertainty in a new relationship. While some firms have begun to use flat fees, most are doing so reluctantly. We do so enthusiastically. Differentiation.

Does any of this compare with, say, Bill Gates's brilliant marketing of software for personal computers or Richard Branson's service-based Virgin brand? Obviously not. But it shows the power of thinking big—which really means thinking of old things in new ways even if you are not thinking up something entirely new.

Remember Gates did not invent the PC. He just helped develop software to make it run, but many other companies also did that. His brilliance was a simple "think big" idea: He was the first to license the software to any PC manufacturers that wanted to use it. And, oh yeah, the product was pretty darn good.

But while many feel Apple's PC operating software was (and is) better, Apple sought to control distribution by allowing it only on their machines. That is why Microsoft eclipsed Apple's success dramatically for a very long time. (It took until 2010 for Apple's market value to finally exceed Microsoft's.) Richard Branson did not invent airlines or good service, his own style and focus on customers made people want to be part of his universe. Because he thought and dreamed big.

The well-known Soup Nazi from the television show *Seinfeld* provides a small lesson. For years an apparent urban legend about a small stand with incomparable soup but an incorrigible owner swept New York City. Turns out it was true; at the stand known as Soup Kitchen International on 55th Street, proprietor Al Yeganeh dished out great soup with bad attitude. A classic episode where the term "Soup Nazi" was used in referring to him gave Yeganeh instant infame. An earlier reference, in the classic movie *Sleepless in Seattle*, provides the lesson. In that movie is delivered the great line "It's not just about the soup."

When you think big, remember: The market need drives the product or service, not the other way around. And also remember that it's not just about the soup.

Are Leaders Born or Made?

Let's try to find out if you are a natural leader and decision maker. In my experience, these are people who like being in charge, enjoy the challenge of motivating others, serve as key cheerleader, understand how to manage by incentive and good communication rather than fear, don't ponder too long on decisions, and have a strong sense of organization. We now take these one by one.

- *Like being in charge.* I used to think, "Who doesn't like being in charge?"—until I discovered that many people do not appreciate the pressure and potential rejection involved in running anything. In my case, I learned that I enjoy leading the show, but this also puts you "out there" for criticism. At its largest my independent law firm had 10 partners and 40 employees, but I was the only one with ownership in the firm, and served as managing partner. This gave me the power to make decisions. However, in many cases it was impossible to make a decision without someone being disappointed. But in all, I knew I would rather be the one making that decision. Only recently, upon joining a larger firm, have I happily shifted to a role where people I trust and have known for a long time are taking the burden on decision making, leaving me to focus on my work, my clients, my advocacy for small business, and my writing. (More about this in later chapters.)
- *Enjoy challenge of motivating people.* There is nothing more fulfilling for me than to see one of my people really rise to a task in part thanks to my efforts at encouraging him or her to feel a sense of ownership in the project or task at hand. There are times when some who didn't have much promise have surprised me because I waited patiently for their moment. But again, there is the dark side—that moment where someone you thought was coming along disappoints or, worse, sabotages something. But if you're a great leader you still come back for more.
- *Serve as key cheerleader.* You realize that your people take their cue from you and you like that (most of the time). If you're a little down, people will whisper, "What's wrong with him today?" Then they will wonder whether

they did something wrong or whether something is wrong with the business, even if the only thing bothering you is you had a silly disagreement with your teenager. So you show up every day appearing enthused and supportive, regardless of your actual mood. I admit to failing at times on this one. But I can also rise to the occasion. We had a dinner for all 40 people in my then-firm several years ago and I gave an impassioned speech about how important our mission is and how proud I am of each and every one of them. People talked about it for a long time after (I think in a good way!).

- *Manage by incentive and communication not fear.* Great leaders are not the ones who yell and scream and scare the bejesus out of people, firing people and then rehiring them, etc. In my decades of law practice I can remember maybe two or three times that I raised my voice. And although I did not share equity with my partners in my prior independent firm, I never made a decision affecting them without seeking their input. Good management is not about sharing power; it's about good communication. If you truly listen to your people and, in fact, take their concerns into account, the appreciation will come full circle. Usually. That does not mean everything has to go their way, but when it doesn't, make sure they understand why. Fear may result in compliance but resistance at the same time. A good leader rewards the good and listens.

- *Make decisions efficiently.* I must have had to make several dozen different decisions a day when I was running my own firm. Many became almost automatic and consistent with situations I have dealt with in the past. Some were brand new and required a little thought. I never rushed into a decision, but I did not dwell on the process, either. Great entrepreneurs know that business moves at light speed, and good decisions need to be made as quickly as possible. Some say "never look back." I disagree. After a decision is made, monitor its implementation so that if problems occur you can learn from them.

- *Have a strong sense of organization.* This simply means being a good planner and organizer. Thinking ahead is critical to good leadership. This is often what keeps great entrepreneurs (well, anyway, me) up at night. Playing all the "what ifs" in your head and determining how to deal with them. But your company should have a clear structure in which each person fully understands his or her role and responsibilities.

Are You Driven Enough?

Now we look at the need for entrepreneurs to have obsessive passion and drive. For good or bad, the most successful entrepreneurs pretty much eat, sleep, and breathe the business. Their minds never stop going and, in fact, in many cases proper sleep is rare.

Once you get "the bug," frankly it is hard to let it go. When I was head of the Wharton School of Business's worldwide alumni association, I met a sophomore who came to me for advice. He told me that he had a great idea for a new business (it was a great idea) and he was seriously thinking about dropping out of school to pursue it full-time. Of course, he could point to famous successful college dropouts such as Bill Gates, Mark Zuckerberg, and Michael Dell, but by the end of the talk I convinced him to stay in school and pursue the dream in his spare time and summers. He thanked me and did graduate several years ago. He recently sold the business after building it for a few years and now works for the buyer.

Where does the passion come from? In my case, what drives me are two things. One is the intense desire for success and the love of not having to work for anyone else. I'm sure analysts could have a field day wondering why that intense desire is there, but this is not *Psychology Today*.

Someone once asked if I'd like to be rich and famous, and I responded that I don't need to be famous. My mood is almost directly a result of whether it's been a good or bad week or month in my law practice business-wise. This has not been the greatest for my wife, who says when I worked for others in a big firm and was miserable I didn't "bring it home" with me. Landing that new client, closing a corporate transaction, or helping a client solve a difficult problem is the only drug I need. I'm on my computer by 6 AM, and as mentioned above part of what gets me up every morning is one of the entrepreneur's laments we'll hear about later on: the fear of all of it going away.

As far as not working for anyone else, I think some people are simply wired to want to have others make the big decisions so they don't have to. They also want more certainty in terms of income, benefits, and the like. For entrepreneurs, we are flying without a net. But where we take the business and how we spend our day, week, month, year, is 100 percent up to us. We get all the credit and all the blame. And we love it—most of the time.

As mentioned, in late 2010, for a number of strategic reasons I combined my practice group with a larger firm. It's a great shop with leaders I've known for a dozen years. They are based in LA and I'm the most senior partner in New York. They are smart enough to allow me to pursue and handle business based on my experience and the mutual trust that we have developed. Thus, while I have the benefit of this larger platform, I really don't feel that I work *for* anyone. We work collaboratively, which is great, and by turning over the management of the firm to them, I'm freer to focus on business development, writing, pleading the case for small business with the regulators, and servicing my clients' matters.

When our youngest started in school full-time, I decided to go back to my prior habit of working from home one day a week. This is not a day off.

In fact it is my most productive day, with calls, reading I have to do, and sometimes just doing some good thinking. And it gives me more time with the family. If I were a partner in a larger law firm, there's simply no way I would get away with that on a regular basis. Even with my new firm, I continue to regularly work from home.

What makes the passion go away for some? That's the big question. In some cases it is the types of things we will talk about in the rest of the book: boredom, burnout, the business growing too bureaucratic, or trouble in the business. Many are facing that in the tough economic environment of the last few years. No prior downturn prepared most of us for what we went through during the Great Recession.

The bad economy has another positive effect: It creates many new entrepreneurs. I've always said the best time to start a new business is in the depths of a recession. Because you have nowhere to go but up.

Are You a Macromanager?

Now let's look at whether you qualify as a macromanager. As I mentioned earlier, this is the antithesis of being a micromanager.

Wikipedia says that *micro*management is where a manager does not allow people freedom to make decisions, which causes the manager to be heavily involved in smaller matters. It often stems from insecurity, but can be the result of a particular corporate culture. Some even say micromanagement can result from neuroses or other emotional challenges.

The best entrepreneurs learn to delegate day-to-day tasks, leaving them to focus on larger decisions, strategic planning, and major problems that arise. If you have a tendency to be a micromanager, can you change? Not clear. Why is micromanagement bad? It breeds resentment and lack of trust. It also takes the manager away from the important things they really need to attend to.

Is micromanagement ever good? In a small business you work very closely with people, so more direct supervision tends to be more common. Also, in tough times where you need to watch every step and every penny, the fact that you presumably can do things better than each of your staff may mean having a little more hands-on approach. In addition, you may find that there are certain employees where closer supervision is simply required, whereas others work better on their own.

Micromanagement is different from being a control freak, although there is some overlap, but we will get into that more in our discussion about control issues.

In general for entrepreneurs, however, macromanagement is more likely to lead to success. Your people will make mistakes. But if they don't learn from those mistakes and avoid them in the future, maybe they are not the right employees for you. If they take a different stylistic approach to things than you do, isn't that a problem? It's only a problem if the style somehow undermines you or hurts the business. Let people do things their way, consistent with your overall business philosophy.

There are risks that come with being a macromanager. I had a client with a key sales executive who was cozying up to the customers, as was his job. Unfortunately, my client didn't realize the executive had a plan to leave a year later to set up a competing shop (after his six-month non-compete) using all those contacts. The client had to bring suit to stop the executive from pursuing these contacts by arguing that he took their contact information from the client. So yes, stay involved enough to minimize the risk of this type of mutiny. But that can be done better by ensuring you retain a strong, personal relationship with your client or customer, not through obsessively monitoring everything the executive does.

In my case, I am probably a natural micromanager, unfortunately. But I have painstakingly trained myself to evolve into what I believe is a very solid macromanager. I did it with an approach I call "Close your eyes and pray." I know that sounds a little flip, and it's really meant more as a joke. I work hard to train my people well over periods of time, and then I allow them to do their jobs with minimal interference, knowing that my clients will be well served by capable and talented people.

When I send out documents for clients or adversaries to review, typically I would state in an e-mail that the documents are attached and for the recipient to contact me with any comments. An experienced former colleague of mine prefers to write rather long e-mails, pointing out important changes or provisions and why they are there, or noting why we did not make certain requested changes. This may not be how I do it, but it does not mean my way is right and his wrong. Did I ever insist that he stop? No. See how well-trained I am?

So if you're going to be a great entrepreneur, macromanage.

Are You a Rational Optimist?

We turn now to rational optimism. Once again I didn't make it up; I discovered there's even a blog by a former judge called "The Rational Optimist." How does the idea apply to building your own business? As noted, the best entrepreneurs charge on, believing all good things are ahead, but simultaneously they prepare for future challenges.

As mentioned, I am a proud graduate of the University of Pennsylvania's Wharton School of Business and former chairman of its worldwide alumni association. But my fellow grads and faculty get a little miffed when I suggest that business school did not complete my business education; law school did. This is because business school classes tend to focus on challenges as a business builds to the stars. In law school we learned about managing risk, something that got little, if any, attention in my business classes.

But neither, on its own, is totally healthy. A successful entrepreneur would have a difficult time if he or she spent the day assuming the worst will happen and therefore avoiding pursuing new opportunities or risk. The best entrepreneurs have no or little fear of taking chances. But doing so cavalierly also does not make sense. The best, of course, is an intelligent balance of the two.

How does this manifest in real life? An entrepreneur who thinks his or her business will only grow might take actions such as highly leveraging the business with debt, since a growing business generally can handle debt service, all without diluting the founder's equity ownership. But if a company is too highly leveraged, a downturn can mean devastation, restructuring, possibly even bankruptcy.

On the opposite side, a company founder who is mired only in fear of bad things happening will do everything in a slow and piecemeal fashion. Take small risks one at a time. This makes it harder to be a fierce competitor if one is in a business where that is required. For example, as mentioned previously, nearly 20 years ago I changed my billing structure in my law firm to more flat fees, rather than billing by the hour. Very few people did it. But I knew it would resonate with clients on many levels. It did. If I feared no one would accept it, I might not have even tried. Now, 20 years later, it is a key selling point I use in encouraging potential clients to work with our firm, clients indeed love it, and other firms are grudgingly putting their toes in the water to try it.

But then how to properly manage growth and build a business while protecting the downside? Well, this is the issue, no? The answer is there is no easy answer. It seems to me the smart way (which I admit I do not always follow) is to take advantage of good times and put away resources for the next challenging time. Yes, you really want that Maserati, but a Mercedes E Class will do just fine, and you put another $100,000 in reserve for the future. But preparing for growth also is important. When I had my own law firm, we managed growth by adding space as we got close to filling space we had. This left empty space, so we rented out offices we were not using, offsetting the risk of taking on the space. Then, as we grew into the space, our tenants left. If growth did not come, the cost would still be managed by the tenants.

And what about when things are bad? How do you time the next upturn? How can you tell how long things will stay bad? Sort of like the last few years for many people. In this downturn, before combining with my current firm, I painstakingly slashed my overhead over a period of about four months. I cut it more than the hit my business took. This meant even if things got worse, I could still manage. But thankfully the last several years have seen a real turnaround in our practice, and a good chunk of the business that was lost has come back.

Do You Have a Healthy Fear of Failure?

Now we move to more personal challenges, first focusing on whether you have a healthy fear of failure, and next, whether you also have little fear of risk. They seem incongruous, but as we will lay out, in a perfect world they are both key elements of an entrepreneur's psyche.

I often say that one is not a true entrepreneur until one suffers a very significant setback. That negative experience can help guide entrepreneurs through both good and bad times. In my case, it happened early. During law school a friend and I bought a radio station in Daytona Beach, Florida. (He and I had run our college radio station together.) We raised money from investors, negotiated the purchase, and assembled a team, all at the tender age of 23. My friend went down to run it while I was in law school. About five years later we finally sold it for a big loss. During that time, we learned a lot about crisis management, to say the least. More about this later.

When things are going great in my law practice, as I mentioned there's a little voice in the back of my head asking, "When are they going to take this all away?" While it does not remove my willingness to take risk, that little voice ensures that I think long and hard before doing so. And when things are not going well, I am, unfortunately, able to draw on the radio station experience in developing strategies, staying calm, and remembering that everything comes in cycles.

I have a business contact who works with wealthy families. He is often asked to advise children or grandchildren who are buying or starting a business. If Grandpa hands you $5 million to do this, in these families the children know very well that there are many more millions after that. So they "play business," as my contact likes to say. They really do not have that same fear of failure that I bring to my law practice. If things don't go well, Grandpa will still be there, and their lifestyle will not be affected. As a result, in many cases these businesses simply do not develop successfully.

This also can be a challenge for a super-successful entrepreneur who may have sold a business or two and has significant so-called "F.U." money in the bank. A client of mine sold his business and pocketed $20 million after tax, in his mind absolutely more than enough to retire on, though he was only 46. A year later he decided to invest $2 million of his now $21 million and start a new business. He certainly worked hard at it, but he admitted to me that he did not have the same drive or passion that he had building the first business: "Not only was I putting food on the table, but it was a scorecard for me, showing where I stand in the world, and it made me proud." Once he had attained a status he was happy with, there was less visceral need to shine, and at the same time very little fear of failure. Sure enough, the new business did not succeed.

Those who become just as driven and failure-fearing despite privilege or significant financial resources tend to focus on the embarrassment factor attached to failure. They are determined to make whatever they do succeed to show the world they are the best at something. Even if they have done it before, as they say, it is all about "what have you done for me lately?" Most real entrepreneurs do not want to hear from colleagues that so-and-so had one great hit but can't seem to be able to repeat it. That fear of failure works for many.

Do You Have Little Fear of Risk?

Sitting alongside the healthy fear of failure, for great success, must be a corresponding lack of meaningful fear of taking risks. The "when will they take it away?" thoughts must be balanced with a willingness to pursue challenges without great trepidation.

The extreme risk-taker, of course, has the greatest chance of falling the furthest. Note the heading of this section is not "Do You Have *No* Fear of Risk?" Those with no fear filter can find themselves too much on the ledge too often. For some, the "adventure gene" that creates endorphins simply takes over and causes them to drive faster, jump out of the plane, and wrestle bears.

How does this manifest? I had a client so certain of the fact that his new company's innovative product would take off in less than three months that he sold his house and most of his belongings (he was single at the time), giving him just enough to pay his 20 new employees for three months. He didn't see the need to raise capital or borrow money. He literally lived in his car for most of that time (his employees didn't know this). When success didn't happen fast enough, he had to fire his employees, move back in with his parents, and take a job at a competitor, where he simply handed them his product as a condition to his new employment. This was a guy without a fear filter.

How simple it would have been for him to either (a) hire fewer people, (b) raise some money from traditional sources (as we will see later), (c) try other methods of marketing his product, or (d) bring his product to market more slowly. But his lack of fear, plus, frankly, his irrational optimism, killed the business before it even had a chance.

It is, however, critical for successful entrepreneurs that their risk aversion level be pretty darn low. In the classic TV game show, *Let's Make a Deal*, the host always asks contestants if they will take cash or the unknown item behind a curtain, which might be a new car or a pile of junk. In most cases they take the unknown item. Comic Howie Mandel brought the concept to modern day with his TV show *Deal or No Deal*, in which the player bets on whether remaining unopened briefcases have more money than is being offered by an off-screen "banker."

In the business world, successful entrepreneurs are more willing to bet on what's behind the curtain or the unopened briefcase. But they hope they can do so with more than a random chance. Maybe blackjack is a better example. In the casino card game, if you study the way experts teach how to react to various card combinations showing on the table, you can dramatically improve your odds of success, even though there remains a high risk element to the game.

Many say that entrepreneurship is often like casino gambling. So many factors outside your control affect your likelihood of success. But, as with gambling, you can train yourself to be aware of those factors, build them into your analysis, and hopefully align them with your personality with respect to fear of risk. If you are highly risk-averse, chances are creating and building your own business is not the route for you.

Can You Control without the Freak Part?

Now-jailed former Enron chief executive officer Jeff Skilling, when asked by his attorney during his securities fraud trial whether he considers himself a control freak, said, "It's more accurate to call me a *controls* freak than control freak." Clearly Skilling did not want the label "control freak." Why is that? Is it bad?

Pretty much yes, but not entirely. Many believe that the "freak" part of "control freak" is the problem. If a leader is obsessed with controlling everything, he or she will focus too much on the least important things and even focus on things that don't particularly help with the business. Think of the theft of strawberries in the classic story "The Caine Mutiny." Ship commander Queeg's paranoia sends everyone on their ship on a wild goose chase to find two shipmates who stole some strawberries. Yes, the control freak often borders on being paranoid. No, we are not here (as I will have to say often in this tome) to provide psychoanalysis of entrepreneurs. But I am thinking just about anything in business that involves being called a freak is probably not good.

I worked with an entrepreneur who spent 50 years building a very successful auto supply business in the Midwest. Both of his children, a son and daughter, both extremely bright and talented, wanted to work in the business. They both came in and quickly found that their father had no interest in having them involved in running or controlling the business, because he could not fathom sharing power, even with his own flesh and blood. He declared them lazy and worthless, and they both left. Only years later when the father became senile did they return and continue to successfully run the business. Besides the effect it had on the family (the children ultimately forgave him), it hurt the business for a period before the children returned when his dementia was not discovered for a number of years.

A leader who takes control is a good thing. It means you are focused. You are keeping an eye on things. You are aware of what your key people are doing and what their priorities are. You do not cloister yourself in your office assuming people are motivated and performing. You jump in during a crisis to work closely in the trenches. You look for fat and waste during good times. You make decisions carefully but efficiently. There's even a blogger who suggests that it's okay to let out your inner control freak a bit.

Is control freakiness different from micromanaging? It can be. Micro-management is not always about control, and control freaks are not just about micromanaging. For example, I may feel the need to more carefully oversee an employee who is struggling (micromanaging) without being a control freak about it. However, if I monitor all my employees' Internet site visits and personal e-mail sent on company computers (control freak), that may not constitute micromanaging.

U.S. President Ronald Reagan was often criticized for his detached style, giving tremendous authority to those around him. But when it came to his relationship with the then–Soviet Union, his focus was to spend great effort assuring that the Communists were honoring agreements made with the NATO allies. But he also felt he had to express respect for the relationship while doing so. His famous line was "Trust, but verify." I have used that principle often in business and in protecting my law clients.

Is Your Life Disciplined?

We will talk in great length later about work-life balance, and the importance of staying healthy and keeping a strong family life. Here we are taking a slightly different focus, namely that of having a disciplined approach to life and business. The streets are littered with smart, hard-charging entrepreneurs who crashed and burned because of their failure to stay focused and disciplined as the business grew.

If you have many or most of the personality traits described so far, in particular a very healthy appetite for risk, it probably means you run headlong into the dark side of being a risk taker. Some are simply born with an addictive personality, which both drives their success and their attraction to things that can skewer that success. How many super-famous celebrities or major entrepreneurs find themselves in rehab? How many are divorced? How many can't seem to get away from Vegas or Atlantic City? Well, not all, and not even most. But while "work hard/play hard" sounds like a good plan, as we will cover more later, it doesn't always get along well with a disciplined approach to work and play.

I worked with a super-successful entrepreneur who built a multi-hundred-million-dollar technology business. Let's call him Larry. We were working on a major transaction for his company. Yet there were periods of several days at a time where literally no one knew where he was. He would resurface and say something about personal matters, and we would continue. This happened four or five times over the six or seven months we worked on the matter. His subordinates had learned to cover for him and say, "Well, that's just Larry." As lawyers, we learned to hold off the opposing side during these times. The transaction ultimately was completed successfully, and Larry benefitted very nicely. I wish I could tell you where he was during those days, but we never found out.

How about a different story? Morty, a survivor of the horrors of World War II, started a business from scratch, successfully building it into a several-hundred-million-dollars-a-year business. When I met him, many years later in his early 80s, he was still the first one in the office each morning around 7:30 AM after a brisk walk in his neighborhood. He kept his mind going with daily staff meetings to ensure that things were running smoothly. He took an occasional glass of wine, was fairly religious, was devoted to his wife of many years, and while a tough boss did build loyalty among his employees. Why? It was because they knew what to expect with Morty. He did not disappear. He didn't don a lampshade or flirt with his female employees at the company holiday party. His personality was relatively even keeled. In all, he was a strong and predictable role model to the staff.

For good or bad, many would-be entrepreneurs bring big personalities to the business. The same passion for excitement in life that brings them to start a business also drives them to have more than that occasional glass, not be so devoted to their spouse, don the lampshade, and flirt with the employees. You might find them in Vegas a bit more than necessary, and so on.

In the mid-2000s, I worked with the CEO of a client in Arizona. It was a health care business and the CEO had built it into a nice sized company. He was passionate about the business, and very talented and loyal to his staff. But all was not quite politically correct. Every year there was a major cigar event for customers, suppliers, and company executives. One year I was finally invited to come to Phoenix. I noticed that the five or six senior female executives in the company were not present. When I asked my client about it, he said he couldn't invite them because it limited his, shall we say gentlemanly fun after the event.

First, let's look at the lesson about the CEO. The business went a little south in part because these personal things were beginning to interfere with the CEO's focus on business. The company faced financial challenges and ultimately went out of business.

Now the lesson about creativity in the face of a challenge. After he told me about keeping the female executives out (clearly a violation of law, as it was discriminatory), I thought about it and tried to devise a solution. The following year they offered all company executives, as well as their customers and suppliers, to go to either of two events—the regular cigar night or an evening of spa treatments at a top Phoenix location. Legal problem solved without simply telling my client "you can't do that." It turned out that all the female executives, and one male, went to the spa, and everyone else went to cigars.

And now the lesson about whom you surround yourself with. I admit that my creative solution was not contributing to increasing the discipline of my CEO's life. But I'm pretty sure that my role as outside counsel to what was then a fairly big client would have been at risk if I had told the CEO the cigar event had to be canceled. This creates another challenge to undisciplined entrepreneurs: They are often surrounded by enablers who depend on them financially and don't want to confront, criticize, or challenge them.

Part of retaining or obtaining that disciplined life is making sure that the advisors, key employees, and other business relationships you maintain help encourage and support that discipline, not the other way around. The challenge is when a relationship that is important seems to require that extra effort.

It is custom in China, for example, that you do not generally gain the business trust of another until you are drunk with them. I had a client who whisked me to the PRC after having read my book on reverse mergers, determined to learn much and have me speak to various groups after having formally hired me. Each night was a lavish dinner, usually with 40–50 people, at which I was the guest "star." I certainly drank some (I stuck to beer) but was generally in control while those around me were, frankly, pretty darn hammered.

The last night I was there was the first night where the translator they provided to me was not their employee. When I came back from the rest room, the translator told me that my hosts were very upset that they hadn't been able to get me drunk yet. I decided that, well, it was my last night and I should respectfully do as they wish. I am told I did some of the best karaoke they had heard that night, and I continued to do work for this client for years thereafter.

But I learned: The next trip, I brought a female colleague who is Chinese with me (women are generally exempt from the drinking requirement). Each night she concocted an excuse as to why I could only have one or two drinks. I had an important conference call with the United States later that evening. At lunch she told them I had to go to an important afternoon meeting. They were not insulted (though they tried every which way to change my mind), and I continued to do work with them. And we still did karaoke!

Therefore . . .

I can't say that I know particular entrepreneurs who have all the qualities described in this chapter (I know I don't), but you certainly need to have a majority of them if you hope to build something big. The thing of it is, even if you've got what it takes, be careful what you wish for. Diving into an entrepreneurial venture involves enormous challenges. The remainder of this book talks about just seven such hurdles that can be faced and how they can either be prevented or repaired.

I remember when we worked on buying the radio station. The process of first finding a station that was attractive and in our price range, then negotiating the business transaction, then raising money for the process, then handling all the legal documentation was quite daunting for two 23-year-olds, including one trying to get through his second year of law school (yours truly). When it was all done and the papers were signed, and we owned the station, we high-fived each other and then suddenly froze. "Wait," we said. "Now we have to actually make this thing successful." Ultimately, as noted, we didn't and I became an entrepreneur with my first significant setback. But I have luckily had successes both before and after, and for me, I wouldn't have it any other way. So if you're ready, let's go!

CHAPTER 3

Staying Focused While Working on New Ideas

Entrepreneurs are natural dreamers, who tend to focus all they've got on pursuing something new and exciting. For many, there is nothing like the adrenaline rush that comes from trying something innovative or risky.

The first book I wrote in 2006, *Reverse Mergers*, was nothing exciting or innovative. But it was the first and remains the only text on taking companies public through alternatives to traditional initial public offerings (IPOs). Not to blow my own horn, but it has earned several book awards, and in 2011 TheStreet.com labeled it "the seminal text on reverse mergers." Never mind that it's the only text; we disregard that little detail.

Writing a book does not seem like a big deal at first. I had chaired several day-long conferences on the subject on both U.S. coasts. At the end of the third one, my good friend Burt Alimansky, head of the Capital Roundtable, who organized the conferences, said, "You know, you should write a book." I said, "Okay." I had no idea what I was getting myself into. It took two sometimes-frustrating years to find a publisher (no, I did not self-publish) and another year of Saturdays to write and edit the thing. No, it was not easy to do with two children living in the house with us, but they were wonderful, supportive, and understanding of the project.

The book finally came out in December 2006. It sold out three printings, was translated into Chinese, and was updated in a second edition, which is also selling well, in 2009. The reverse merger industry is not that small; about 200 reverse mergers are completed each year (more on the industry and its history a little later in this chapter). There are certainly those with more experience than I who could have written the book. There were several who told me that they were thinking of writing the book, or had even written a few chapters. But I was the guy who got it done.

It's pretty clear that it now makes no sense for someone else to try to write another book on ostensibly the same topic. What's the point of all this? I not only had the dream to do the book, I actually followed through and did the hard work to make it happen. It has been a tremendous source of business for my law practice, spawned my blog (which is visited by thousands of professionals each month), and frankly has significantly enhanced my reputation as an expert in the field. And it's all because I stuck some words on a page. So much is about turning the dream into reality.

In Comes the New Idea

Much like the songwriter who has new tunes popping into his or her head all day, often entrepreneurs are creative types who are constantly thinking of new ideas to pursue. Remember sad, old Ralph Kramden and his unending hope for the "big one."

Successful entrepreneurs know how to dream, and then how to make it happen. But as they're making it happen, what if a new dream develops? While successfully building a business, an entrepreneur may come up with something additional that may be accretive to the business that is already there or, sometimes, may be an entirely different business altogether. This may be especially true in the current challenging economic environment, in which entrepreneurs are apt to sense the need to diversify or hedge their bets.

Remember that entrepreneurs are the ones who never listened to the advice "Don't give up your day job," since most of them did exactly that. I'm working with an entrepreneur client now who is getting ready to leave his pretty lucrative full-time job. He was running the new business from home, at night, and on weekends, and is now ready to take the plunge. But what if a great new idea comes just months or a few years into the new venture? How do you ensure that your first business doesn't slip while you dive into the new obsession? Or should you even do so? Ah, that is the conundrum we will now explore with some real-life and some semi-fictionalized examples.

The Complementary Business

A client of mine had a rapidly rising magazine business. He was on the *Inc.* magazine list of the 500 fastest-growing private companies. At one point, he got excited about adding a business conference side to the operation that he felt would complement the magazines. He could promote the conferences basically for free in his large circulation magazines, then make money selling sponsorships and attendance fees for the conferences. In turn, the conferences would bring more business and advertisers to the magazines. Again, it was something that had been done before, but not in his industry.

He got very pumped about the conference business and focused almost exclusively on that. He told me he hadn't been as excited and focused since he started the magazines 10 years earlier. He felt the magazines were successful and left relatively inexperienced managers to tend to them. They simply were not the visionaries that he was and were merely somewhat capable caretakers.

Several years later, he began to realize that the magazine industry he was in was consolidating, and that his larger and larger competitors were beginning to crush him. He returned his attention to the magazines for a short time, but by then it was too late. The conference business also was not developing as successfully as he would have liked. Both attendance and sponsorships were lighter than expected. He also learned about the cash flow challenges of putting on conferences. You have to spend quite a bit of money to get them organized, but money does not come from attendees until right before, or in some cases months after, the event.

So he put his company for sale as magazine revenues stopped growing and the conference business was losing money. After a year with the company on the block, he finally ended up selling the business for much less money than he had hoped.

Was it wrong to have tried to get into the conference business? Not necessarily. He later admitted that his mistake was taking his eye off the base business of the magazines while doing so. He said that in hindsight he would have hired a strong, experienced manager for the conference business, and he could split his time between that and keeping the magazines going. Why didn't he do that? He was so excited about the opportunity he felt no one could pull it off as well as he could. And he wrongly believed he could succeed with the magazines essentially on autopilot. He abandoned his base.

Following the King of All Media

How can you pursue the new idea the right way? You will hear a great deal in this book about one of my business heroes: controversial radio "shock jock" Howard Stern. While he has not built a company, he has built a brand in a real entrepreneurial fashion and made a fortune doing so. Stern complains incessantly about having to get up at 4 AM to do his daily radio show, now down to three days a week around 40 weeks a year.

So why not give it up to do something else? He has written bestselling books. He has put out top-rated videos. He had one of the most successful pay-per-view events ever televised. He has produced TV shows. He has a very successful "on demand" cable channel, mostly video replays of his radio show but also including original content. He had a wonderfully successful movie adapted from his first book. He has even said that making the movie was one of the happiest times of his career. The self-proclaimed "king of all media" can do and has done it all.

Stern often chides celebrity guests who walk away from lucrative franchises, like the star of a hit TV show who leaves to make movies that flop. He looks at stars like Charlie Sheen and Lindsay Lohan and is puzzled as to why they self-implode right when they are on top (again, we are not psychologists here and clearly that is part of the issue). He feels they should milk the success for all it is worth and never give up their base.

Most believe Stern will retire at the end of his current five-year contract in 2015, and he probably signed this last one more to protect his staff and give them time to find new opportunities than to enhance what one assumes is his already-sizable (though presumably divorce-depleted) estate.

Recently Stern became a judge on NBC-TV's talent show *America's Got Talent (AGT)*. A brilliant business move even if creating more exhaustion in the life of the self-described "tortured man." It was brilliant because it was all completed during his time off from the radio. And because he convinced the producers to move the already-successful show to New York from Los Angeles to limit his travel. Because talking about *AGT* on his radio show has been very popular, fans love hearing about backstage gossip and the like. Because the initial success of his takeover of the show (although there are two other judges, he is clearly the standout) brings millions of new possible subscribers to his satellite radio show on Sirius/XM. Because he dove into the new project without ignoring his main moneymaker (radio). And because it helped soften his "bad boy of the radio" image to show his caring side, and to show that he can be funny and edgy while also being clean in his comedy. This might be setting the stage for his next gig after he finally retires from radio. And, oh yes, he reportedly received $20 million to do it.

And most importantly, it is brilliant because the multi-millionaire superstar still gets up at 4 AM three days a week to do the radio show, his real meal ticket and his base of success. He could have changed the radio show to go on later in the day (his daily show replays all day anyway, as he has his own channel on satellite radio). He could have tried to move fully to cable TV, or make more movies. But he knew that anything requiring him to give up the radio, take his focus away from it, or give up being live during critical "morning drive" time was a mistake.

So unlike my magazine/conference business client who took his eye off the ball and suffered for it, Stern only takes on new challenges that fit well with his continued focus on his 30-plus-year success on the radio. So the lesson is not to avoid new challenges while building your business and protecting your base; it's looking to do so carefully, strategically, and while maintaining your focus on the original source of success.

Not Just Reverse Mergers

There are times when sticking only to the initially thriving business can be limiting. In my case, I had become known as a lawyer helping companies go public through non-traditional means such as reverse mergers. As mentioned, I have written the only text on the subject (*Reverse Mergers*) and travel the world for speaking engagements. In a reverse merger, a company goes public by combining with an already-existing public company that has no active business. We call this public company a shell company. The process is much simpler, cheaper, and quicker than a traditional initial public offering (IPO). Plus most companies below about $200 million in value cannot even attract potential underwriters of IPOs to take them public, yet many of these companies can benefit from a publicly trading stock and have the financial ability to bear the cost of doing so.

While reverse mergers have many positive features, in the 1970s and 1980s there was a great deal of fraud in the space until the U.S. Securities and Exchange Commission (SEC) made some regulatory changes that improved things. Unfortunately in the late 2000s fraud was also alleged in several dozen Chinese companies that went public through reverse mergers, and the SEC passed some additional restrictions on these transactions that have recently reduced the number of transactions being completed.

I have worked very hard to lift up the image of this technique and encourage legitimate players to do things the right way. I have worked with the SEC to improve some of the more egregious regulatory burdens. I also encourage the use of other alternatives to IPOs, including a so-called self-filing with the SEC that has become more popular as the regulatory burdens on reverse mergers have increased.

The "IPO alternative" part of my practice remains a key foundation to my success. It is clearly what I am best known for, thanks to the book, my blog, and appearances at conferences. It is greatly appreciated when I am referred to as a thought leader in this area, and, in a nod to Howard Stern, some call me the "king of reverse mergers." In a good way, I hope.

However, this area of my practice never represented even half of what I do as a corporate and securities lawyer, and these days even less so. It just happens to be where my notoriety came from. This was both a great source of business and, in some people's minds, a limiting factor. "I think of you for reverse mergers and didn't even realize you do other things" was something I heard more than once. Of course, when I would hear it I would set the person straight. Since for many years my name was on the door of my firm, many simply presumed that we were a "reverse merger shop." Nothing could have been further from the truth.

I do many other things, and I believe I do them very well, too. I have many years' experience helping companies complete venture capital investments into their business. I do ongoing work for public companies after they complete an IPO or reverse merger. We handle traditional IPOs as well as public offerings that are completed after a company is already public, a so-called secondary offering. I work with startups and other private companies in structuring their ownership, capitalization, and basic documentation. I handle "corporate divorce," where partners are splitting up but without litigation. And these are just some of the other areas in which I have been able to develop expertise and work with clients.

I have also been very active as an advocate for small business with Congress and the SEC. I speak at and attend SEC-organized conferences on microcap and smallcap stocks. I help shape legislation and rulemaking. This gives me unique access to the mindset of the regulators that I believe gives our firm a leg up in advising clients.

I am also very experienced in mergers and acquisitions (M&A). In fact, it's one of my most favorite and challenging things to do. Why? Because I have developed a reputation as a good negotiator, often able to overcome limitations on my clients' leverage to obtain a better result than one would normally expect. How do I do that? Well, I think I have to keep that one from getting out. But I enjoy the process of negotiating key elements of an M&A deal.

I also enjoy M&A since I am often on the "sell" side, helping an entrepreneur get rid of the business. We will be talking later quite a bit about when and how to sell your company as it grows. The M&A deals allow me to dust off the four psychology courses I took at the University of Pennsylvania as I advise entrepreneurs who are effectively selling one of their children in an M&A transaction. I am as much counselor as scrivener in these situations, and I enjoy the challenge.

While the portion of the bar that is focused on reverse mergers is relatively small in terms of competition, the number of attorneys handling M&A is tremendous. Every large law firm worth its salt has a major group devoted just to M&A. Many big firms are happy to work on smaller transactions of the type that I would "pitch" for, and their marketing machines can be pretty effective and daunting.

But I realized that I cannot limit my reputation to just IPO alternatives, even as I make sure to "protect the base." And this seemed to be a logical area to attempt to expand my reach. As one M&A guru said, I already do mergers; people should also think about me for acquisitions. In a reverse merger there is an acquisition of a shell company, etc. So thanks to the success I have had with the book, my blog, and appearances, I was able to "jump the line" a bit when I decided to become more visible in the M&A world.

What does this mean? For example, because of my work and also my former role as chair of the Wharton School of Business's worldwide alumni association, a very prominent M&A networking group invited me to join the board of its New York City chapter. Normally it takes years of dedication to the group before they make such an invitation. But because of my prior notoriety, and ideas I could bring from my work with the Wharton alumni network, I came right on and stayed on the board for three years.

And even though I had no real M&A reputation, an M&A trade association invited me to speak several times at its major conference, which attracts 500 people. I initially spoke on reverse mergers, but the second time talked more broadly about the regulatory environment for small and midsized companies.

This brings me to note that my advocacy work is also getting noticed beyond the IPO alternative world. I am active in helping push for all regulatory changes that benefit smaller companies, and clients are beginning to notice the value of that involvement in our dealings with regulators on their behalf. This also allows me to broaden my reputation beyond just reverse mergers.

I've done a number of other things to get out of my reverse merger comfort zone and get the message out about other capabilities. Frankly, one of the reasons I decided to combine my practice with a larger firm was so that people can come to me and say, "Okay, now that you're in a firm that is known for these other types of work we can send you that work as well." Forget that I always could have done that work and done it well; the perception with some was that my focus was only on IPO alternatives.

How do I spread this word? One example: I got an idea about five years ago from an accountant friend who used to organize a "law firm managing partners group" that met quarterly in his office to talk about issues of running a law firm. Of course, his goal was for us lawyers to send him business, in particular litigation support business that accounting firms do. And it worked well, though my friend has since retired.

I woke up one day and realized that I know five of the managing partners of major professional services firms in New York. Why not try to do the opposite and get these professional service managing partners together? When I talked to one or two of them, the initial reaction was "Well, we see each other at national conferences. We really don't need anything like this."

Somehow I convinced the five to show up for breakfast at my office one day (we now have seven and have decided to keep it small). Within the first half hour, we all knew something special was happening. I try to always have a topic to discuss, but frankly the men (yes, all men) come into the room and just get right into whatever it is they have to deal with at the time.

I learn so much from listening to these men, who collectively oversee probably 8,000–10,000 employees. But I also get the chance each time to talk about what my firm and I are doing and promote us. When a client going public asked to be referred to professional service firms, I called three of the managing partners, and they brought their A-list partners to meet my client. More importantly, these guys now know the full range of my firm's and my capabilities—"not just reverse mergers."

So, as you see, I have spent time increasing my visibility in M&A. This has led to some great new client opportunities, including a multi-hundred-million-dollar sale of a client several years ago.

As I write this I am getting ready for the eighth time I will be speaking at the annual major reverse merger conference. Thankfully I no longer have to chair these events, as a different conference organizer, DealFlow Media, has taken over producing these gatherings. More about DealFlow and its founder, Steven Dresner, later in this chapter. I am staying at all times focused on the base, never turning down a reverse merger speaking opportunity, and continuing to build visibility through my blog, www.reversemergerblog.com.

Even the choice to move forward with this book, with its much broader potential audience appeal than my first book on reverse mergers, is part of this strategy to let folks know that my capabilities are much broader than my base. Get it?

The New Idea Relieving Boredom

What are a few situations where taking on a new challenge may not make sense? Later we will be talking about the challenge of boredom that can develop with some entrepreneurs, particularly as the business grows and becomes less entrepreneurial. We will discuss strategies to stave off or deal with boredom. My magazine/conference client was in part victimized by this. He was not yet bored, as his company still had a real entrepreneurial feel internally, but he missed the excitement of something new, and that was one of the key factors that drove him to his major focus on the conference business, ultimately unsuccessfully.

I had another client whose new company was a sports-related business I incorporated, and then helped him through several rounds of financing. We subsequently took them public through a traditional IPO when revenues hit $32 million. Through some smart line extensions and quality products, the company managed to grow to $100 million in revenues in just four years.

I could begin to tell that the CEO was bristling at the bureaucracy he was forced to impose on his growing business. He had little patience for meetings, occasionally disappeared for hours on end, and seemed distracted. He also didn't notice that much of his growth was being financed with increasingly expensive bank borrowings. To put it simply, he was bored. But as long as the business was growing, debt service did not seem to be an issue. And the business was doing well, though growth slowed a bit as the CEO's focus seemed less intense.

His board was beginning to be a little concerned about his reduced passion. Right around this time, sure enough, a new opportunity arose. It involved a very innovative new product that he strongly believed could revolutionize his industry. Suddenly he was in the office around the clock, focusing on the new product. He was newly energized, very excited, and very determined. Some of his colleagues said he finally seemed like his old self. He tapped out the company's credit line to its maximum to finance some research and development. The board was cautiously behind him since they were pleased he was "back in the saddle" of being intensely dedicated to company business.

So what happened? After nine months of expensive development, including the leasing of additional space, it became clear that the new product would not likely be able to be launched without significant additional funds. The company's debt burden made it basically impossible to convince investors to buy stock from the company, and no more debt was available. The board had no choice but to suspend the work on the new product.

The CEO was dejected and upset. He tried to devise other ways to finance the opportunity, but it was to no avail. He once again became more reclusive, and less and less involved in overseeing his managers. When the business began to drop, the lender declared a default in the debt, and this caused the company to file for bankruptcy and ultimately liquidate about a year later.

Was it wrong for the CEO to have tried to take on the new opportunity? Well, he was probably wrong to commit so much of the company's resources and risk capital to it all at once. He probably did this more because it gave him something new and exciting to work on than because it truly made the most sense for the long-term success of the company.

In hindsight, board members told me they made a mistake "coddling" the CEO for his "pet project," and they should have insisted that the company continue its upward trajectory on its main business and not take this outsized risk given the strong position it was otherwise in. And, they tell me, they probably should have insisted on a professional CEO to complement or work under the founder since his focus was gone.

Taking on a new project in an otherwise-successful enterprise primarily because of founder boredom is probably a mistake. If it is to happen, ensure that it does not put the rest of the company at any inordinate risk.

The New Idea after Years of Grooming Top Deputies for Main Business

There are situations in which you have less worry about moving forward with a new project or new initiative or new passion even as the main business continues to thrive. For example, Microsoft founder Bill Gates was truly the driving force behind the success and growth of his company. For a long time he was an autocratic taskmaster, personally involved in virtually every decision that mattered even a bit. As we will discuss later, he bypassed boredom in part because of his tenacious determination to crush or acquire everything in his way. As we know, of course, the company grew to one of the largest businesses in America.

Gates spent years bringing on and grooming key aides whose trust he developed and who were truly talented emissaries of the Gates business philosophy. Did they have the same competitive drive that brought his success? Maybe not 100 percent, but enough. Executives like Steve Ballmers and others were continuing to build the business very successfully with Gates able to spend less time on day-to-day matters.

Then, a new opportunity brought itself to Gates—not a business opportunity, however, but the chance to make a real difference in the world through a major philanthropic initiative. He and his wife would travel the world promoting the Bill and Melinda Gates Foundation. He gives stirring speeches on how poverty can be significantly reduced by helping poor countries do a better job of farming. He didn't just put a bunch of money into a foundation and hire someone to run it. He has extreme passion and has dived into this work with what appears to be the same intensity that he brought to building Microsoft. And with his tens of billions committed, he really can make a difference.

But should he have taken his eye off his Microsoft "base"? He remains chairman of the company but is no longer its regular spokesman. He is much more focused, it seems, on his philanthropy. In fact, he refers to it as his second career. Once you have tens of billions, why care at all about the original company? Why not just be retired?

Gates is clearly not retired from Microsoft. And he was able to pursue his new opportunity for all the right reasons: He spent years building a strong team that could continue to build the company and innovate without his regular involvement. He still cares about the company's success because it will always reflect on him. His timing to move on was based on his effort to ensure that his first love, Microsoft, was ready to manage successfully without him. And he gets all the excitement of pursuing something new without putting his original business at risk, the mistake my sports guy from earlier made.

Is this an extreme example? Maybe it is. But scale it down and this could be any successful entrepreneur who has made even $10 or $20 million, if he or she prepares company number one for life without him or her before moving on to the new opportunity, whether it is being pursued inside or outside the original business. My magazine/conference guy didn't do enough to protect the main business before taking on the new opportunity.

The New Opportunity Following Financial Success

When else might it be okay to dive headlong into the new opportunity? When you have had so much financial success in the initial business that even its failure would not damage your security, you're good to go. Of course Gates is an example of this, although I think for him the importance to his ego and legacy remained very high despite his dramatic financial success.

I had a client in an entertainment-related business. After working hard for 20 years to build his business, he had already taken out close to $30 million that was clear and in the bank—in his mind, more than enough to assure him and his (second) wife a very happy life, regardless of whatever else happens in the business. The business remained successful, though he was a little burned out from the long hours it took to retain that success (more about burnout later in the book).

Sure enough, a new business opportunity arose in a completely unrelated business (biotechnology). He loved the idea of making money while helping mankind, versus his prior business of entertainment. The company had a potential drug that could help wipe out an illness that had taken a close family member of his.

He decided to invest $3 million in the new business (still leaving him a fortune to live on) and asked a longtime vice president in his entertainment business to take it over while he still retained majority ownership and served as chairman. He joined the biotechnology company as chairman and co-CEO along with the founder who had brought him the opportunity.

His former VP did a great job continuing to build the business (it was eventually sold successfully) with his chairman level oversight. He and his co-CEO of the biotech company managed to develop the drug far enough that a major pharmaceutical company bought it three years later. He got $10 million for his original $3 million investment.

A great story of course? Of course. Do they all end up this way? No (see some of the stories from earlier in this chapter). This was a win-win. He did well in the sale of his original business and left it strong enough for his focus to go elsewhere, allowing him to do some good for the world and make a huge profit in the process. So, yes, there are times and situations where the moment is right to allow an exciting new opportunity to take over your drive.

The New Opportunity as a Hedge

Are there other times when diverting your focus is worthwhile? Ask my friend and contributor to my previous book Steven Dresner of DealFlow Media. Quite the impresario, Steven was the first and only player in the small and microcap stock markets to recognize the need for information to be available about ongoing transactions and trends in reverse mergers and private investments in public equity (so-called PIPE transactions).

He started documenting the not-yet-multi-billion-dollar PIPE business in the semi-monthly *PIPEs Report*. It was delivered to subscribers who eagerly awaited the news of deals completed, which firms were growing in the space, and who was getting into trouble. They also coveted top spots on his PIPE "league tables," listing who was doing the most deals and who was doing the largest deals. He then decided to add a semi-annual PIPEs Conference, but, unlike my earlier client, put the right professionals in charge of both the newsletter and the conference, allowing him to split his time between them. The PIPEs Conferences, along with the newsletter, were a great success during a period where the transactions really flourished, through about 2009.

Also during this period he realized that a similar approach can be taken for reverse mergers, a smaller market than the many funds, investment banks, and other players in the PIPE business, but ripe because there was no other resource for information. So was born the *Reverse Merger Report*, but only *after* he did a very successful Reverse Merger Conference. Again, talented folks running while he oversees.

In looking down the road, before things got bad in the markets for both PIPEs and reverse mergers, Dresner believed that his dependence on just these two types of transactions had great risk of a dramatic downturn, depending on the markets and the regulatory environment.

So what came next? For a time their report on special purpose acquisition companies (SPACs), a particular type of shell that became very popular in the mid-late 2000s, was a big hit. But when those transactions went dormant in mid-2008, so did the report. But DealFlow still holds a SPAC conference at least once a year as SPACs have slowly come back in 2011 and 2012.

He has also added coverage editorially and in some cases through conferences of registered offerings (IPOs and other public offerings), smallcap equity finance, turnarounds and restructurings (great hedge, which will be busier in a market downturn), life settlements (growing in popularity), and the newest addition, crowdfunding. All of these are areas of interest to small and midsized companies and those that advise them.

So for Steven, the "next great idea" was a broad one: keep adding strategically worthwhile coverage areas to hedge against the base. Sure enough, the PIPE and reverse merger markets have been hurt in the last few years. So he has combined three different newsletters into one weekly *DealFlow Report*, which covers all those topics. And he combined multiple conferences into one major one.

What did this mean? When the markets went down and his business should have been potentially irrevocably damaged, he readjusted those areas and, more importantly, kept the newer areas, a bit less market-sensitive, going strong to keep feeding his bottom line.

He was able to do this without taking his focus off his base by taking some, but not all, of his attention and depending heavily on strong people to take the lead. This creates some risk, as at least one senior manager left to start his own competing newsletter, but Steven was smart enough to keep strong deputies under each manager and was able to replace the departing leader without much difficulty.

Why was it important—indeed necessary—for him to add these different business areas? Because his main business was very risky and cyclical, and needed to be balanced with other opportunities that were accretive to the business and counter-cyclical or somewhat non-cyclical.

When the New Thing Is Bigger

What if your current business is pretty solid but either not growing, at risk of being challenged by competitors or simply not overly profitable? What if a new opportunity then arises that has the potential to dramatically dwarf what you have built over a number of years but has never met your expectations? Do you walk away from what you built, which is okay but not fabulous, or leave possibly inexperienced or non-visionary managers to run it? Do you keep focus on the base, and split your time?

More importantly, even if you are going to consider effectively abandoning your existing company, what criteria should you use to determine the potential upside of the new opportunity?

This is not like my entertainment guy, who already had $30 million in the bank, or Gates, who spent a very long time grooming his successors. Here's an easy example, Howard Stern again. After decades in terrestrial radio, having built a syndicated morning radio show heard in dozens of cities, Howard felt frustrated by the growing restrictions on his freedom. The U.S. Federal Communications Commission (FCC) had fined him multiple times, things he could have said earlier in his career were now verboten, and the censors were having a field day "beeping" out things as he was saying them live on the air.

A former boss, Mel Karmazin, had joined a fledgling satellite radio company called Sirius. Not everyone could receive the station; you had to subscribe and, at least at first, listen only in your car with a special radio that had to be installed. Once installed, you could hear the station wherever you went, unlike terrestrial radio, where you lose the signal when you leave its base city. But the coolest thing: no FCC oversight, and no restrictions on what he can say or do on the air. He would finally be free.

Of course the details of Howard's discussions with Karmazin are not publicly known. But Stern had many millions of listeners; estimates were close to 20 million at the height. His pay also was not public, but reports were that he was making around $20 million per year on terrestrial radio. Equally important, *he was influential.* Everyone talked about what Howard said or did that morning; even haters couldn't help but listen, the way one has to watch a train wreck. Yes, he was often vilified in the press, but his loyal fans would do anything for him. Why walk away from being the biggest thing in radio ever and millions of dollars for this hugely risky venture?

Two things apparently did it: money and freedom. His first five-year deal, starting in 2006, was reported at $500 million in total. That apparently included the costs of his show and staff, but if you start at $100 million a year, one assumes he was taking home much more than his prior $20 million. Plus there were various significant stock incentives tied to reaching a certain number of subscribers. Reportedly, the first bunch of stock he got and promptly sold netted him about $200 million. As this is written, Stern is suing now Sirius/XM claiming he should have received credit for the XM subscribers that came aboard when the two satellite radio companies merged. Some have criticized him, asking: Doesn't he have enough? He says it's about right and wrong.

And what about the freedom part? Well, his show today is much like a trip to a high school boys' locker room, and strippers and porn stars come on and do crazy stunts. The language is about as coarse as one might expect. But he also has great guests like rock legends and TV celebrities, often getting them to open up about their personal lives in ways that no other interviewer seems able. And frankly, many men don't mind sitting in their car on the way to work taking a sentimental journey back to that locker room (or ladies imagining it).

Does he still have 20 million listeners? No. Did he acknowledge trading that for freedom (and money; he doesn't usually acknowledge that on the air)? Yes. I'm sure he wishes he could have 20 million listeners on Sirius. But he did give up his "base" on terrestrial radio. Maybe he surmised that radio is radio and he was just moving the base. He took a huge bet that his fans would pay to hear him, and the bet paid off as he signed a second five-year contract in 2010.

What's the lesson for us here? He took a major risk in terms of his reputation and notoriety, knowing he would probably end up with fewer listeners. For many entrepreneurs, that risk is part of the excitement. Plus, unlike someone starting a new business, his financial security over the five years was assured, as was his cherished freedom.

So if that new, possibly bigger thing comes along, will you have the assurance that Howard had that it will pay off financially? Assess new opportunities very carefully before tossing aside something that is okay for a dream. Oh, wait—that's what you did the first time. But remember your first dream, in this scenario, didn't work out quite as you expected. So make sure to bring some serious analysis to the new opportunity.

Sell That Sucker

Another thing to consider when the new bigger thing rears its head: Think about selling your current business before moving on. We will talk more about "serial entrepreneurs," but suffice to say successful repeat business owners know the right time to get out and think about the next project.

Let's imagine a hypothetical situation to help explain. We lawyers love "hypos." Why make something up? Because you may recognize some of yourself here, and aspects of this and other hypos in the book are taken from real clients and friends of mine. Hopefully my hypos will be both entertaining and illustrative and lead you to say, "I resemble that remark."

Susie and Katie start a business just after they leave college, where they both studied business administration. Let's say it's an online system for ordering bagels delivered to a college dorm room or fraternity or sorority house every Sunday morning. They enlist students in various colleges to pick up the bagels and make the deliveries, and they partner with bagel stores to get it done. They hire technicians who make sure the student employees are fed the necessary information about orders. After two years they are available to 20 colleges and are bringing in nearly $1 million in revenues.

Even though they hire additional people to help expand into other colleges, they seem to be doing everything themselves. They get some nice press both online and on some cable news shows (Susie and Katie are very attractive and speak very well), but sales are not expanding as quickly as they did the first two years.

What are some of the challenges? Their customer base is not very loyal, as up to one-fourth of them graduate each year. There are not great barriers to entry, at least at individual colleges, and competitors, run by students in three of the schools, start to appear. They have nothing proprietary about the business that can be protected such as intellectual property, although their name, "Bagel Chix," does get some attention and has developed some cachet.

Their profit margins are not large. Even though they attach a handsome markup to the cost of the bagel with students knowing they pay a premium for the dorm delivery, after costs of the "runners" and marketing expenses each has earned only about $25,000 in salary in year two. Their management team is thin, and it is difficult to attract experienced executives to such a small business with very little to offer in compensation.

The model does not lend itself well to franchising, since the amount to be made in one school alone is not that significant. They can think about expanding their product line (they added drinks and thought about donuts), continue expanding to other schools, etc. There is one key employee, Courtney, hired in year two, who turns out to be as dedicated as they are. Courtney happens to be from the wealthy Smythe family of Westport, Connecticut, and just got excited about the bagel project when she met Katie and Susie at a bar one night. She was between jobs and took a chance on the girls, figuring she had nothing to lose.

While Courtney remains excited, Katie and Susie are frustrated by the problems outlined here. They think the challenges to build the business to a significant level are overwhelming. Right about this time, the girls get an e-mail from Percy, a friend from college. He tells them that he showed some of their TV appearances to his father, Mr. Abrams. Abrams is a TV producer and has been developing a TV show to be called *Emerging Entrepreneurs*, or something like that. He has been looking for two attractive unknowns to host the show, which will focus on different young entrepreneurs. He expects the show to air on a major cable channel, and has produced four or five successful shows in the past.

Abrams has the idea to bring in the girls to host the show. They can talk about their own bagel experience as they find and interview other up-and-comers. Abrams's problem is he has a limited budget, and so he offers the girls the chance to host the show as a full-time endeavor in exchange for part ownership of the show itself, a very rare opportunity. If the show does well, it could mean easily hundreds of thousands of dollars for these young recent college grads.

What to do? The girls feel like they didn't go to business school to host a TV show, but it's a show about business, and they can be entrepreneurial in the endeavor through their ownership. But what about Bagel Chix? It's their first endeavor, and they hate to just shut it down or let it go—but they know they can't live on $25,000 a year and know the challenges of building from there.

Luckily, their star employee, Courtney, overhears their dilemma and immediately contacts her dad, Mr. Smythe. Courtney believes the business is scalable, and she and her dad decide to offer the girls $150,000 to be paid over three years to buy the business, the online site, and the name. They will get $50,000 up-front.

They go for it. The $50,000 helps them in the first few months of the show, and after they impress Mr. Abrams so much, he adds a $30,000 stipend for each of them. What happened? Well, this is a hypo, so how about we say that the girls each made $200,000 and then went on to become TV producers themselves, and Courtney hobbled along with the business and grew it to $3 million before selling it herself for $500,000 and joining a major national consulting firm?

What do we learn from this made-up (not as much as you think) set of facts? First, life doesn't always turn out how you thought it would in school. Second, when your current endeavor's challenges are significant and a new, potentially larger one comes along, consider a sale of the first company rather than trying to do both or abandon one. It worked out for Katie and Susie!

Therefore . . .

Hopefully you leave this chapter with a number of tools to utilize as an entrepreneur when a new project is seeking your focus—some dos and don'ts if you will. Don't take your eye off the base if the base is solid and performing, even if you are bored. Do consider a new opportunity if you have made your fortune, if you have spent years grooming your successors to continue your business success, or if you have the ability to divide your focus intelligently. Do consider going ahead if the newer project is accretive to the business or a hedge against your current business's risks. If your current business isn't that great, or a new opportunity is that much bigger, consider abandoning your current endeavor or consider a sale of the first company if possible. Be sure to carefully analyze the new project before giving up on the old.

In sum, while that Great New Idea needs a lot of attention, in many cases you should not obsess over it at the expense of continuing to bring the same dedication, enthusiasm, and creativity to your main business. Focus on the base and save 2–3 AM for the new idea.

CHAPTER 4

Getting a Life

How to Have a Business *and* a Life

I don't really like the phrase "work/life balance." This is mainly because it implies that work is not really part of life. Maybe it should be "work/off-work," though that doesn't exactly roll off the tongue. I told an associate recently that I was taking the next day off. She said, "Is there really such a thing for you?" This is the unfortunate state of affairs for many people—entrepreneurs in particular. So maybe it should be "work/less work."

For many entrepreneurs, for good or bad, this work part of life becomes their entire life. Some people are born workaholics, and others ascend to that lofty place. In today's plugged-in world it becomes even more difficult for already-jazzed-up business starters to move to the "less work" part of their life. What are the advantages and disadvantages of focusing on nothing but work 24/7/365? What strategies do successful entrepreneurs enlist to fight the urge to avoid their "less work" sides?

The Downside of Workaholism

I spent my early years as an attorney working in several large law firms in New York City. I got tremendous training and experience, and stay in touch with many colleagues from that time. The large firms do offer the highest pay and you leave with great contacts and a "pedigree" that follows you.

But the lifestyle of lawyers at most big law firms is pretty grueling. One hundred–hour weeks are not unusual. Young associates know not to make solid plans in the evenings since it is more likely than not that they will be stuck in the office. Maybe they can meet a friend for a drink at 10 PM. Maybe. Weekends are also not totally safe; walking around any big firm on a Saturday almost looks like a regular day, except everyone is in jeans.

It doesn't get much better if you get the brass ring and make partner. I know a 45-year-old partner in one of these firms who lives in New York City with his wife and two teenage sons. I asked when he gets home at night, and he said usually around 9 PM. But it's okay, he says, because his kids are older and they're up at that hour. I asked if he works on weekends, and he said, "No, just Saturdays. Sundays I only work at home." To him, Saturday isn't even part of the weekend. It doesn't seem to hit him that he's basically telling me he works seven days a week.

I was already married by the time I started in these large firms, so luckily I was not looking to have time to make dates and hopefully find my soulmate. Most of the 20 and 30-somethings earning their keep in these firms want to do just that. It is one of the reasons so many of them eventually choose to move in a different direction, even if for less money.

How do people survive it? There is this concept of shared misery among coworkers that makes it a little less unbearable. If we're all sitting together in the firm cafeteria at 9 PM eating ordered-in Chinese food and joking around, it takes some of the edge off.

Here's a secret: I am not a workaholic type. I have always been very ambitious, determined, and hardworking, and have been very blessed and lucky to be successful. But I also believe that life is too short and prefer not to sacrifice any part of my life, no matter the benefit. Later we will talk about some of the strategies I have used to find balance, including developing a terribly efficient way of getting things done.

But in these large law firms, especially at the partner levels, people survive because you tend to find a high percentage of all-out workaholics. These are *not* the "work hard/play hard" types we talked about in Chapter 2. These are folks who always seem to believe that there are simply not enough hours in the day to get everything done and they will have to stay in the office for all hours just to make a decent dent in things. Even when work is not that busy, they find low-priority projects or take their existing work to even more depth.

There are generally two types of partners in law firms: service partners and rainmaking partners. The service partners oversee the work that rainmakers bring in. The service partners' main value to the firm is their ability to work hard and supervise others. Thus many feel that putting in extra hours and weekends is a big part of what they bring to the table. But the truth is, some just prefer it that way, regardless of whether it's required. And for the most part the rainmaking partners like that they are this way.

Again, let's distinguish between a hard worker and a workaholic. Hard workers put in the time because they have to or believe that's what is necessary to achieve, but they would much rather have at least some "less work" time. Some might work hard to avoid whatever awaits them at home. Workaholics *get satisfaction* out of living, breathing, eating, and (not) sleeping work. They simply can't stop themselves from continuing to work—hence the word being tied to addiction.

There are some good things about being a true workaholic if you are an entrepreneur. Presumably, you get a lot done. Customers, suppliers, and others can rely on you to perform and be accessible. You have extra time to analyze things in more depth than you might otherwise. You set an example of putting in many hours as a model for your employees.

But what else can happen? A client of mine started a software business at age 25. He was married at the time. He was a true workaholic who lived at the office and on planes. What happened? His 24/7/365 work brought great success to the business, and he was able to take tens of millions of dollars out of the business to build a substantial net worth.

But there was a downside: His marriage fell apart when his wife felt like a widow who never saw her husband. Luckily they had no children. He lost focus because he was always exhausted and didn't notice after 15 years at age 40 that his industry was changing in a way that ultimately forced him to shut down (luckily with all that money in the bank). He developed heart problems because he had no time for exercise and was often stuck eating fast food because he simply didn't have time to do otherwise.

So what is the downside of workaholism? It can lead to less focus, less efficiency, less productivity, and, like with my client, even health problems. Not to mention, in many cases, it can simply lead to unhappiness. With rare exceptions it is a fact that the quality of the work a workaholic does at 1:00 AM is not as good as the work he does at 4:00 PM. And like it did for my client, it can lead to destruction of whatever personal life you may have had, including time with your significant other and kids.

It is true that these are the same results that come from simply being a hard worker who would rather not be putting in all the time he or she does but feels it necessary. And you can add in that it can lead to resentfulness. What can happen to an entrepreneur facing these challenges? He or she is super-motivated about the business but misses being with his or her family or just taking time off. If he or she is not careful the business becomes more of a burden in the entrepreneur's mind than the exciting new opportunity he or she started with.

In addition, these challenges are typically harder for female entrepreneurs, because women tend to feel more responsibility for child-rearing. If they have workaholic tendencies or simply feel they have to work hard to pursue their dream, they may feel even more sadness than men at being away from home. And of course if Mom is not around at all, even for some "quality time," it is likely to affect the children negatively (see: fictional character Meredith Grey on ABC-TV's *Grey's Anatomy*, whose famous surgeon mother was never around and ended up having affairs before Alzheimer's took her mentally from her children).

In June 2012, the *New York Times* ran an article on entrepreneur moms. The upshot of the piece: Venture capital firms all too often discriminate against female entrepreneurs in making investment decisions, particularly if they are pregnant or have children, suggesting this may be part of the reason that only 10 percent of entrepreneurs are women. Is this fair? No. But it is an unalterable fact that only women can become pregnant, bear children, and breastfeed them. So is it understandable that investors consider that fact in deciding what companies to back? I leave that for you to decide. In particular, they suggest that a female entrepreneur taking two to three months off after having a child can have a real negative impact on the business.

Regrettably, this is a real concern. But it shouldn't stop venture money from coming into these companies. The key is for the entrepreneur to work an arrangement to convince the investor that the company will not be negatively affected. In some cases a partner or strong deputy can pick up the slack. Some can take only a very short time off and then head back to work with good nursing help at home. Others can do a great deal from home during leave.

The problem with this view is you can extend it to all work. I once worked with a partner in a large law firm who would not let me add a young female attorney to my team on a new important client. He had praised her work previously, and I thought it would be a no-brainer. Why not add her? He said (he really did), "She can't work on this big client because she's going to leave here and have babies." I explained that this 27-year-old had a boy-friend but was not even engaged, much less considering children. It did not sway him. That really happened.

Let's get back to workaholics. So how do you go after that ladder to success as an entrepreneur and avoid being "Uncle Daddy" or "Aunt Mommy" who only sees his or her kids on Skype as they're going to bed? Can you be there as a mom for every soccer game and school presentation? Can you find ways to enjoy life during your "less work" times? The answer: maybe, if you respect the difference between *working hard* and *working smart*. Let's explore that now.

Tips for Working Smart

When I started my own law firm after my seven years in large firms, for the first time I was in total control of my schedule and my day. I described it to friends as having a "s**t-eating grin" on my face all the time. What I quickly discovered was that it was not so easy to figure out exactly how many hours a day to devote to building my practice. I had a wife and a young child at the time, and enjoyed being with them. I enjoyed vacations and day trips and exploring new places. But I had taken this giant leap from my high-paying job and I was responsible for providing for them. (My wife was not working at the time.) So I knew I had to do everything I could to put all my effort into the new firm I had started with one partner.

I later told people that the dilemma works thusly: You can spend 100 percent of your time at work, and you can spend 100 percent of your time at home. Now figure it out. What were some of the things I did? How did some of my entrepreneur clients find their balance?

Time Shift!

As a lawyer, I have never put in as many total work hours as I have in the last few years. This is for many reasons. As a published author, I am in demand for speaking around the world. I am spending six months of Saturdays writing this book. I am a senior partner in a growing law firm. I am overseeing my client matters and practice group. So how do I have time for my now-11-year-old son (my older daughter is in college) and wife?

Time shifting. If my son has an event at his school at 9:00 AM, I make sure not to schedule anything that would conflict with it. Most entrepreneurs have enough control of their schedule to do this. Sometimes there are challenges. For example, I remember a time when I was slated to be a speaker at my son's elementary school graduation (I was vice president of the board of the school) to be held at 8:30 AM for about 90 minutes.

But wouldn't you know it, the big annual Reverse Merger Conference in New York was scheduled for the same day. I was also supposed to be a speaker there, and the conference organizer wanted me to moderate the morning session. I couldn't miss that conference (remember not to forget the base!). I just didn't see how I could get from my Long Island home into the city in time.

I was really frustrated and didn't know what to do. I finally solved the dilemma by requesting the conference organizers to switch me to speak on an afternoon panel. I got to the event shortly after 11:00 and only missed a little bit.

Saying no has also been a challenge. If my son is performing in his winter concert at 9:00, but a client also requests to meet at that time, I'm sorry, but I will just have to work with the client to set another time. Is everyone this way? No. But one of the major benefits of entrepreneurship is the freedom to structure your own schedule and not be a slave to a boss who requires you at work all day every day. You do not have to sacrifice your ambition for this; just make up the time somewhere else.

Time shifting. If I have a big reading project for a client but it needs to get done on the same day as that winter concert, I will either get up at 5 AM to do it, or get to it later in the day or after he goes to sleep at night. I won't miss the concert. And my project will be completed. Working smart.

I know a successful salesman with five children. They are all in college and grad school now (yes, imagine the cost of that!), but when they were small, he didn't miss a recital, science fair, or birthday party at school. He caught up when he needed to at night, early morning, or, if necessary, during the weekend.

Is this just about kids? No. You can apply the same philosophy to other "less work" times. You want to get a massage, play an hour of tennis, or hit the gym? Time shift. Pull that off and you can put Uncle Daddy on the shelf. More about "me" time below.

Delegate!

Here is another way to address the negatives of over-work. I do something that is often hard for entrepreneurs: I delegate. Yes, I know many entrepreneurs hate the "D" word. But it is critical not only for helping a business grow, but also for creating some semblance of a true work/less work balance for the entrepreneur. As we said in Chapter 2, the macromanager is much more likely to find success than the alternative.

We will talk at length later about the best way to find the right employees for your entrepreneurial environment. For our purposes here, accept that no one will do things as well as you do, and work on finding ones who can do them well enough. Our focus will be on finding the right team that can execute and allow you to focus on the big picture, key hires, and new initiatives. But they also help you with your ability to add some "less work" time.

My wife runs a children's summer day camp near our Long Island, New York, home. The camp has over 600 children, 250 staff, and 16 staff supervisors who report to her. During the eight summer weeks that the camp runs she has tremendous help from her very dedicated staff. The first year she ran it, in the off-season she had no help at all. She was really enjoying the work since she loves children, but there is a tremendous amount to do between camp seasons: recruiting families, finding and interviewing hundreds of possible staffers, planning the schedule, arranging trips, conducting monthly supervisor meetings, ordering summer program supplies—oh, and did I mention recruiting families?

That first year off-season she rarely left the office before 10 PM and was there pretty much seven days a week (on Sundays they schedule tours and interviews). Family members and I shared taking my son in the evenings. Luckily he attends school where the camp is, so he could do his homework with her in her office after school. But it was a very stressful time because of her having to work so hard (she is not a workaholic but a determined person who always gives 110 percent to any project) with a child at home.

The first summer she was there she was very successful. She made it an absolute requirement of returning that she add full-time, year-round administrative help in the office. Now she still remains in the office until 6 or 7 and goes for Sunday morning tours, but she is much happier with the help she is getting and able to spend more time with the family. Also, she is happier at work, more focused, and less frustrated. She is therefore more effective in her job. And the following year she added a second full-time administrative person.

This is a small example involving just the addition of one person, but illustrative nonetheless. For me, I work hard to train young attorneys in my shop to take on responsibility as soon as they show ability to do so. As a business grows, you will find that your ability to oversee everything dissipates. Without the ability to put strong people in and give them authority to get things done, that growth will by nature be limited. In addition, it provides more ability for you to have more "less work" time.

This does not mean that you abrogate supervisory responsibility. Back to good old President Reagan: "Trust but verify." Make sure your people provide you with regular reports, and maybe even copy you on e-mails, and do some spot-checking on your own.

Remember why this is important: It will improve how you approach business. It will enhance your focus, your productivity, your happiness, and your efficiency. And it will help you remember that life is not just about work, even when you are building an entrepreneurial venture. An old adage: No one on their death bed ever said, "I wish I spent more time at the office."

Work from Home . . . Sometimes

In most jobs the idea of working from home is still pretty unusual. And it is interesting to note that at the time of this writing a number of major companies are curtailing or even eliminating "telecommuting." But if you are an entrepreneur, you can do whatever you want. You control not only when you work (time shifting) but where you work.

A client of mine—let's call her Stephanie—lives in Los Angeles, and owns and runs a small investment bank. She is indeed a hard worker (thankfully not a workaholic) and is successful. She has a team of about a dozen people in a beautiful office in Beverly Hills where she keeps an eye on everyone from her corner office. She is determined to keep building the shop, which has doubled in size in just the last two years. Her days in the office are pretty crazy: one meeting after another, running to this place or that, and quite a bit of travel.

Stephanie has a 6-year-old daughter and an 8-year-old son who attend a local public school where she lives in Santa Monica. Her husband is a dermatologist who works in a local medical practice. The kids have a wonderful babysitter who takes them to and from school, and watches them at home after school until Mom and Dad come home.

Stephanie also loves tennis and had become quite adept in her younger years; before getting married, she even played on her high school tennis team. She never has enough time for it, given how busy she is at work and taking care of the kids. When her kids were babies she would be lucky to play a few times a year.

About a year ago, once the kids were both in school full-time, she made a decision. Every Wednesday she arranges an 8 AM tennis lesson or game, and then works from home the rest of the day. Sometimes she even sneaks in a manicure.

Of course, it doesn't always work, as there are sometimes meetings that have to take place on a Wednesday. But she is extremely busy and productive at home, because her staff is not constantly stopping by with questions and the phone isn't ringing all day. She gets conference calls done, is on e-mail all day, and can sit and read something for work without interruption.

She likes the 12-second commute. Sometimes if she's a little less busy she stops at 3:30 when the kids come home to spend time with them. Otherwise the kids understand that Mommy's working upstairs and they stay with the sitter. And most interestingly, she told me it has provided some reflective time for her. Sometimes, she said, she sits down in her backyard mid-day just to ponder issues affecting her business and write down some thoughts. It is much more difficult to do that sitting in the office or when you are home with kids running around.

Working at home is not a day off—quite the opposite. But working at home is not for everyone. If you will feel distracted by that stuff in your bedroom you needed to clean up or feel the refrigerator constantly calling you, or if your kids will be less tolerant of leaving you alone, then it may not be an ideal solution.

In addition, much depends on how things are in the office when you are not there. If the staff sees your home day as a day to take it easy in the office, then you have a problem. You have to be at the point of believing that the staff is just as (or mostly as) productive whether you are there or not. Or trade that reduced productivity for the enhanced focus and perspective you get by working from home.

When I started my first solo law practice, I hired a part-time associate who worked specified hours at an hourly rate. He worked at a secretarial desk, so when I did work at home I told him he was free to use my desk and computer to have some ability to concentrate in my office. At the time I could access my office computer through a good old modem and special software so that I could open documents and work on them at home. "Remote desktop" was years away.

I knew the associate was busy and had lots to do. I had frankly forgotten that he would sit in my office when I dialed up to download a document I needed to work on. The software worked by displaying on my home computer whatever is up on the screen in the office. What popped up? The computer version of the card game solitaire! He was being paid by the hour and had work to do. We had a big talk and he ended up staying with me for years thereafter.

Occasionally when I work at home I slip into the office unexpectedly in mid-day just to get a sense of what is happening. I have been very blessed over the years to have dedicated staff who work hard regardless of my presence.

Work Hard/Play Hard Can Be Dangerous

I must admit that I lean a bit in the direction of those who work hard and play hard. It's a natural outgrowth of my philosophy that life is short and to be enjoyed at all stages. I know I need to work hard to achieve my business goals. But I also enjoy my free time (though in recent years have enjoyed less of it!). It helps me recharge and be more focused.

I have been lucky that building my business network has been primarily the process of making friends. As a result my "play hard" time is often with friends with whom I do business. Dinners and outings are as much fun as they are beneficial for business. It has just turned out that way—as I said, lucky. So one trick to working hard but not missing out on enjoying life is to do fun things with business friends.

As mentioned in Chapter 2, however, there are entrepreneurs who have a driven, even addictive personality that drives them, among other things, to work hard on the business. Workaholics put all of that aspect of personality into their job, with all the downsides discussed previously. But there are some for whom a variety of addictions is not uncommon. Work, drink, gambling, and carousing too often go together in entrepreneurs. The danger, of course, is that the darker addictions take over their lives, risking destruction. As discussed in Chapter 2, the key is to find a way to a disciplined life that successfully balances work and less work.

More Vacation with Less Work . . . and More Howard

A number of years ago when my children were young I made a decision to try to take more vacation than I had been. How could I possibly do that? I needed to work every day to build my business. But I realized I needed the recharge that only a trip away can bring. A family trip is not as relaxing as a no-kids vacation, but it's more relaxing than just being home!

So my decision to add more vacation included a pledge that I would not ignore my clients when I was away. I felt being away more was worth the possibility of one to three hours of work each vacation day. I try to allow associates and junior partners to handle as much as they can when I am away, but there is always at least one client or project that requires my personal involvement. When I can be on a conference call sitting by the pool at a nice resort, or read an agreement sitting on the beach with a cigar, I can think of worse things.

Another vacation trick was managing time differences smartly. For years we spent several weeks each summer in Hawaii, where the time is six hours earlier than at our New York home. What did I do? Got up at 6 AM, found a comfortable lounge by the pool, and opened my laptop to check my e-mails from where it was already noon. I was busy with that as well as a few calls for several hours while the family was still asleep.

By the time they made it down for breakfast around 10, the day was nearly over in New York, and when we hit the pool at 11, e-mails slowed dramatically because it was after 5 PM. The entire afternoon and evening were truly free, and yet I handled all the day's business.

On a trip to London we learned that the opposite can be problematic. There it is five hours later than New York. This meant that while the morning was quiet, business interrupted the afternoons and evenings. Of course, we still had a great time, but had a little less time for fun.

My business hero Howard Stern also does it right. His trick to getting more vacation without hurting his business model: developing creative things to do on his Sirius channels when he is away. For decades the model when disc jockeys are on vacation was either to have someone else sit in for them, or to play replays of old shows.

Howard changed the model. For example, for several years he has done "The History of Howard Stern," a wonderfully produced look back on his 30-plus-year career, with tapes of his earliest days and commentary from celebrities and those on his team. Maybe he puts in three to four hours of time taping thoughts and listening to the plan, and then feels better that he will be away for two weeks at Christmastime while his listeners enjoy great new programming.

Stern also manages to fill the days he is not there each week. Every Friday is a show called "Best of the Week" in which the most interesting parts of the show from the past week are replayed. Usually they are great interviews or, yes, it may be some porn star or the Octomom doing some adult things. Listeners enjoy these since they don't always end up at their radio at the moments when these shows are originally aired.

He also creatively developed the Howard Stern news team when he moved to satellite radio. There are about a half-dozen "reporters" whose sole job is to get stories about the world of Howard and report them. Many of the news team's stories relate to the so-called "wack pack," a motley crew of folks with issues of some kind or another whom he makes famous by allowing them on air and, frankly, being somewhat politically incorrect. But when Howard is away, the news guys keep us up to date on things happening in the Howard vortex. Recently his sidekick, Robin Quivers, had a tumor on her bladder removed, and the news guys kept covering things about it even when Howard was not around. It kept the listeners feeling there is always new and current content on the channels even when Howard is not there live.

Other greats that have run when he is away: "Fight Week," in which great fights on the show are replayed and analyzed, another week's tribute to the late comedy great Sam Kinison, and another just highlighting the best moments of the show since moving to satellite.

"Me" Time Strategies

What are some additional ideas for adding more "less work" time to our lives? The previous section focuses mostly on adding family time. What about time for you? Do we have time for work, family, and personal fun or relaxation? *Yes!* In this section we talk about some suggestions that my clients and I have employed.

Is it necessary to add "me" time to your life when you are building a business and trying to also have time for family? *Yes!* Why? Because family time is rarely relaxing time. It may be fun and, of course, fulfilling. But studies show the average entrepreneur is in his or her late 30s, right at the time when young children typically are in the house. So time with kids is soccer games and dance recitals, throwing a ball in the backyard, video games, and tea parties. Even on vacation, as noted, you're having fun with kids but not focusing as much on relaxing. So how is it possible to find time for yourself?

First you need to make sure you know what you enjoy in me time. Some like a nice cigar. Others love to read. A round of golf is preferable for others. Sometimes it is the simplicity of a nap, a massage, or even a mani/pedi. Some love a nice long run, or to take in a new (or old) movie. A glass of wine watching TV for a bit or reading a magazine. Playing in an adult softball or basketball league. A walk in the park. A sweaty workout at the gym, or some yoga, tai chi, or meditation. A nice dinner with your significant other, or a drink with a friend who is unconnected to your business network. A little shopping never hurts. Some have wonderful hobbies like building model airplanes or knitting.

A good friend (over 50) with his own medical practice has a huge model train set that he painstakingly built himself, and also a full music room where he plays trumpet and drums along with prerecorded music. Others like to gather with a few friends and play cards. I have friends who are determined video gamers. I personally enjoy listening to music to relax. I know folks who literally recharge with a break at their favorite coffee place. Another good friend loves to ride horses.

The greatest challenge for an entrepreneur is making an effort to get your me time. Some purposely schedule it. That makes sense. "Oh, I'll try tomorrow" is not the best way to make sure you have the time you need. Like my LA investment banking client who scheduled her tennis game every Wednesday morning, me time requires discipline and determination to achieve.

Me time activities can be of varying lengths of time. A relaxing bath helps many and can be as little as 15–20 minutes. Stepping outside for a walk also does not need to be long. But 18 holes of golf kills an afternoon. Many entrepreneurs feel they simply do not have time for these things. Others have even more guilt with me time as they do finding extra family time, since the business, they feel, needs them. It's not right, they think, to do something so selfish.

Get over it! It is okay—née critical—to take time for yourself. Keep remembering that the business will do better with you enjoying some down time. And it doesn't need to interfere with what you need to do in the business. Here are just a few ways to make it happen.

Finding Less Work on Business Trips

I have an entrepreneur client who loves golf. But he rarely has time to play with small children around, and he is constantly running to their soccer and lacrosse games on the weekends. His business takes over his week, so he never gets out to play.

He travels about every month. About two years ago he decided that on certain business trips he would add a half-day, bring his clubs, and play golf, usually alone but sometimes with people he had visited with on his trip. He found it wonderfully relaxing and of course a little frustrating, as golf can be. But it helped make him happier and, in fact, more productive the rest of the time.

Not a golfer? Try to at least sneak in a massage (or two!) while business traveling. Try a facial or other spa services usually available in decent business hotels. Maybe find an hour or two to do some sightseeing wherever you are. Go take a long workout in the hotel gym. Take a nap! Me time.

In the classic 1989 movie *Look Who's Talking*, George Segal's character, Albert, has impregnated his love interest, Kirstie Alley's character, Mollie. He promises to leave his wife and be with her. She then sees him kissing another woman. He admits he has left his wife but then added, "I know this sounds awful, but I'm going through a selfish phase right now."

Every entrepreneur needs to be a little selfish at times. We all need to recharge (though probably not the way Albert did!). This is even more the case for female entrepreneurs. There's a classic sweet children's book called *Five Minutes Peace*. The Large family is a little crazed when Mom decides to take refuge in a bubble bath to just get a small break, but she never gets it, as the kids keep interceding. Try hard to avoid feeling guilty if you just need to get away and, as the kids say, "chillax" just a little on your business trip.

I do enjoy a nap on the weekends, I must admit. And I do love my 11-year-old son, Andrew, who is just awesome. But he seems to think that a nap just means Dad's right where I want him to hit him with questions, or permission for something, or to tell him the cool thing I just saw online. Repeat: I adore the kid. But the naps I sneak in when I travel have no such interruptions. No dog barking, no phone ringing, no wonderful and well-intentioned 11-year-old saying, "Hey, Dad."

Can the business afford you adding a little extra time to some trips for yourself? Yes. You may find yourself doing some worthwhile brainstorming while getting a massage or just hitting the hotel hot tub. And you'll recharge for what's next. We will talk about the risk of burning out as an entrepreneur, too. These strategies can help you reduce the risk of losing your business because you simply don't have the energy or drive anymore.

Get off Your Butt!

Speaking of energy and drive, "I don't have time to go to the gym" is a familiar lament. My answer, especially for an entrepreneur, is that you have time for whatever you want to make time for. We don't need to repeat here the zillion benefits you get from exercise. Well, okay, I will repeat them: live longer, feel better, lose weight, get more energy. Okay? I admit I have been on the six months on and a year and a half off approach to hitting the gym or treadmill. It so happens as I write this we are in an "on" phase.

How do I have time? I go around 6 in the morning. I'm up anyway and that was time that I used to sit at the computer and deal with overnight e-mails or write new blog entries. But for 45–60 minutes about four times a week, I walk really fast and do weights. For the first time in my life I actually look forward to the gym. I watch some TV and listen to music, and the time passes while I sweat. Me time. And I still manage to deal with the AM e-mails and get my blog entries in.

Everyone finds their way to exercise, but find it. If you have a treadmill at home and you're not too tired at night, you can work out while watching the latest episode of *America's Got Talent*. Even an after-dinner constitutional helps. Just move. And ideally, get your heart rate meaningfully up when you do.

The Early Weekender

My son is a late-night kid, and when there's nothing important to do the next weekend morning, we let him stay up, which leads him to sleep late. I'm up early no matter when I go to bed. So I have a guilty pleasure. There are a number of silly network TV shows that I enjoy, most of which are inappropriate for my son to watch. I tape them on the DVR during the week, and lay in bed on early Sunday mornings and watch them. Paying attention to other folks' drama and comedy does help me escape a bit from the troubles of the day.

My friend with the trains is the same. He has a little conductor's hat, and he gets up early on the weekends to work on adding something to the setup or just run the trains around. If you ask why he loves it, he will tell you his family was too poor growing up to afford trains, and he always wanted them.

Another entrepreneur friend is an avid reader. She reads before bed and in the morning, especially on weekends. She tells me that it gives her a break from all the challenges of her business and being a very involved mom to her two kids. This super-bright, super-talented, and motivated woman particularly loves trashy romance novels.

So when the kids are sleeping, me time can plug right in. Also, don't forget to try to make the most of those rare moments when you don't have the kids. If they went to a birthday party, or have play dates with another family, or have a sleepover, use that time for yourself. As I write this, it is summer and a number of our friends' kids are at sleepaway camp. They miss the kids tremendously, of course, but it allows them a good amount of me time for the gym or whatever they enjoy. When the kids return, the parents are a bit less burned out and recharged not only for business but for continued child-rearing.

For older folks whose kids are grown or at least in college, or who have chosen not to have children, much of this is different. Me time has to be balanced with significant other (SO) time. This is frankly a bit easier to do, assuming your SO understands and supports you having even a small "selfish phase." But it still requires that balance. For many couples, they have waited a few decades to get back to just having each other. So you still may have to get up a little early on the weekend for your time because your SO has scheduled a lovely Sunday brunch out.

Turn It Off, or Mostly

About a year ago I did something that changed my life. On my smartphone I changed the settings so that when an e-mail or text arrives, nothing happens. No buzz, no vibrate—nothing. I check it often, but I check it when I check it. My clients are very well served, and they are better off if I don't turn into Pavlov's dog reaching for my phone one second after every one of the 400 e-mails a day I receive on average arrives.

How does this impact me time? It means when you are trying to have your downtime, business will not interrupt unless you want it to. If I am at the gym from 6 to 7 AM, it is okay if any e-mails that come in during that time wait for me to finish. One time during a massage on a trip I forgot to turn my phone off and it started ringing right in the middle. It turned out not to be important, but it certainly jolted me back to reality just when I was hoping for a recharging period.

Smartphone management is important not just during me time. If you spend your day being constantly interrupted by new e-mails, it will be difficult to get many things done. Some say you should discipline yourself to only check your email once each hour. There are times when I am in a meeting or on a call and cannot check for an hour. If I have an important reading project, I take scheduled breaks to check messages and e-mails, but I don't watch the screen incessantly in order to ensure I don't break my concentration.

I read online about an entrepreneur whose husband turns off and hides her phone Friday night and returns it to her Monday morning. Her key staff have her home phone number for emergencies. She is much more relaxed and appreciates the mental break. It also allows her me time to be more effective. To be honest, I can't imagine doing this. But my response may wait until I've enjoyed a movie with my son, or hit the gym or taken just a little nap.

Therefore . . .

Life is short, folks. Even if you absolutely love the work you are doing building a business, you still need a respite. For reflection. For fun. For refueling. For your health. And to ensure that you are more likely to have good things to say about your choices on your deathbed one day.

If you are a workaholic type, hopefully an intervention can be avoided if you force yourself to go against type and take that break. For some selfishness is simply anathema. Find a way anyway. I have several personality challenges being a transactional lawyer. For example, I admit I am not naturally organized. My brain is more focused on problem-solving and creativity. But as a lawyer I have trained myself to be very organized. In addition, I am now at the point where very capable, anal attorneys that work with me keep our deals and documents extremely well-organized. If I can do that, you workaholics can do it, too.

Work smart and don't sacrifice any part of your ambition, but make that family and me time part of your routine. In this extraordinary economic climate, with all the challenges most of us face in our businesses, we need all the recharging we can get!

CHAPTER 5

Employee Management 101

It's easy to find good people to work in an entrepreneurial company, isn't it? The job market is always a challenge, and any job you offer will lead to hundreds of applicants eager to work hard and please an emerging entrepreneur. It will be easy for you to sift through those hundreds and find the person with the right background and the right personality to match both the job and the culture in your company, and you will bring aboard a loyal team with a positive attitude who are just thrilled to be in your presence. Right?

As my tone implies, it is actually not at all easy to find the right people to work in an entrepreneurial company. It is actually pretty darn hard. Remember the entrepreneur is someone who wanted to stop working for others. So do you hire people like yourself? Wouldn't they also be unhappy working for someone else?

Do you hire drones who are just content with their paycheck and do not care about the scrambling you may have to do twice a month to meet payroll? A conundrum for sure, and each entrepreneur has to carefully examine what type of person is best suited for what is hoped to be an exciting ride to success.

I believe one of the least admitted challenges entrepreneurs face is finding and keeping great people. Let's face it: What do employees of entrepreneurial ventures typically have to deal with? Either they have a micromanaging, controlling boss, or the opposite—one who is not interested in any details because he or she is always "chasing the dream." In the following chapters we delve into how to find the right partners and investors in your entrepreneurial company. As critical as those roles are, equally so is figuring out what it takes to bring in the right people and develop them into satisfied, long-term employees.

Is It Really That Important?

Aren't employees just pawns that can be replaced about as easily as dealing with a dead car battery? Why spend a lot of time talking about getting the "right" people since eventually the right ones will come along and great people will be drawn to your exciting company? I think one of the reasons entrepreneurs have so much difficulty finding and keeping great people is that they do not spend enough time searching for the right people. They just want to fill a job as quickly as possible so they can move on to more interesting things.

I had a client in the fashion business who kept replacing his sales director. None seemed to last more than five or six months. As soon as one would leave he would direct his senior vice president to bring him two or three candidates within a week, since he didn't want any time without a sales leader. The senior VP would hurry to run ads, speak to headhunters, and find whoever was available. My client would then hire the one who seemed least objectionable and hope for the best. Then rinse and repeat six months later.

This is the wrong approach. In any business, large or small, putting an effort into recruiting talent and keeping them satisfied is extremely important. But in an entrepreneurial organization it is absolutely critical. In smaller companies each employee is an important add, not only in terms of the skills he or she brings but the attitude and contribution to the excitement and fun that can only be found in a fast-growing company. How he or she interacts with fellow employees and you as leader can be just as important as the employee's capabilities and talents.

I have been an employer for 20 years, and in that time I have learned that in many cases attitude can be even more important than ability. A capable person who is a diva or divo, exuding arrogance, making demands, and sniping at coworkers, significantly diminishes his or her value, despite job performance. A bright and book-smart talent with zero personality who never interacts with anyone and doesn't leave their desk also may not be the right fit.

Often the most challenging is a super-talented, amazing performer who is a bit too conniving or even manipulative in achieving his or her goals. Yet a marginal worker who constantly goes the extra mile, puts in 110 percent, never complains, is a team player, is outgoing and friendly, and jumps in to help when things are difficult can ultimately be more valuable.

In addition to putting in great effort in hiring, it is equally important to focus on how you treat your people. You may make great hires, but if they don't feel appreciated and motivated, you may not be able to get their best, and in the worst case, they move on. Even when the job market is tough and they are "stuck" with you, dissatisfaction and resentment will build if they do not feel treated well, and that is likely to affect their job performance.

Some entrepreneurs have trouble feeling like they should have to please those whom they have hired and who owe their jobs and livelihoods to them. We will discuss the many ways to provide meaningful benefits to employees easily, and often at little or no cost.

So yes, Virginia, it really is that important to make a priority in an entrepreneurial environment of finding and retaining a strong, motivated, and satisfied employee group. Some of the best approaches my clients and I have found over the years follow.

Finding the Right People

Let's start by discussing how to find the type of employees who will be right for your entrepreneurial venture, then later move to how to keep existing employees motivated and satisfied. Searching for talent in a relatively new or fast-growing company is not exactly the same as finding employees in, say, a small retail store or, at the opposite extreme, a large company.

The difference in a growing entrepreneurial company is that typically the business is either just getting started and frenzied, on a wonderful tear and frenzied, or struggling and frenzied. Does a small retail store or a large company get frenzied? Sure, but not all the time. In most growing companies you might as well put a plaque labeled "frenzied" on each employee's desk.

The implications of a frenzied, highly uncertain business life on finding the right employees are many. For example, for most positions the idea of basic 9–5 is pretty much not going to cut it. You are, as we described previously, either a (hopefully recovering) workaholic or a hard worker making things happen. You will still be the first one in and the last one out most of the time, but in most cases (other than low-level administrative people) nobody will be able to punch a time clock.

What does this mean as you search for great people? You should be looking at folks who will actually enjoy the crazy ride that is an entrepreneurial company and who actually like the excitement of the unpredictability of it all. Maybe even borderline workaholics, but remember the downsides discussed earlier.

How do you find these types of people? By spending time with them before they are hired. Interview them at least two or three times before making a final hiring decision. Try to delve into their personality, not just the contents of their resume. And be as straight as you can in terms of what the position is really going to be like. There's no point in doing a bait and switch and letting someone think that the work is going to be different than you actually expect. Let people know what you will be looking for, and hopefully there will be enough people willing to give it a try.

You may want to try to find candidates who actually worked in entrepreneurial ventures previously. If they did, learn about their experiences, what they liked, and what they did not like. If the "not likes" are similar to what they may experience with you, then you probably move on. If they didn't, try to get a sense of what they think working in this type of company will involve.

The Hire from the Big Company

There is often a temptation in smaller companies to bring in someone coming right out of a big company. There is no question this can work out great. But you need to prepare him or her for the change. As my law firm was growing we brought in a number of lateral partners right from much larger firms. It certainly took some adjusting.

One partner we brought in (this was about 10 years ago) was still not as computer literate as we would have liked and had depended on assistants to prepare documents from his handwritten markups. When I told him he could have an assistant if he paid for it, he said, "I guess I will learn how to type." While it took quite a number of months, and he never got much past "hunt and peck," he did fine, and realized the benefit and efficiency of doing the typing himself.

Several of the folks we brought in had no clue how to use a copier. They figured it out. And ultimately they saw the benefits of having more freedom, less politics, and the excitement of being in a pretty fast-growing enterprise. Not everyone adjusted. Several partners ultimately found their way back to larger firms.

Similarly, a foreign client was setting up a Wall Street operation in the United States. Although they would be operating in the small and microcap markets, they felt the prestige of bringing in folks who had backgrounds from the largest investment houses was important. The problem was they had no experience in the smaller end of the market, and though their compensation was structured to incentivize them, their ability to find and execute business opportunities, despite their many talents, was limited.

So yes, the temptation to bring in people from bigger companies can be great. You want to say, "And meet Brittany, who just joined us from General Electric, where she managed a unit similar to our business."

Brittany may indeed be bringing useful experience and training that would have been hard to find in a smaller company. She could bring practices that cost the big company a great deal to develop, and the smaller company could never have done on its own. Especially as an entrepreneurial business grows, adding appropriate infrastructure and, yes, a bit of bureaucracy becomes more important. As you can see, there can be a real benefit to adding these people.

Just make sure you let them know what's coming before they arrive, and try to get a sense if their personality is a good fit. As we will discuss, I admit I truly chafed in the big firms in which I worked. It's not their fault; I just wasn't built for that kind of environment. I was ten zillion times happier once I started on my own, even without the big firm "safety net."

Of course, you can never tell for sure in advance how people will actually perform when they arrive bright-eyed and bushy-tailed on their first day with you. In my experience I have seen it all: hires that I wasn't sure about turning out great, and fantastic interviews that led to someone coming aboard and crashing and burning. That said, I think one of my few talents is finding talent. That's because I take a lot of time before I make any hiring decisions. And I try hard to be straight and direct about what the job will really be like. That's because I've seen the other side, as the following story will indicate.

My Law Firm Experience

Disclaimer: in some ways this is a combination of several experiences so no particular firm is implicated here! When I was a young lawyer and changing firms on one particular occasion, I made clear that a main reason for my move was to be in a more entrepreneurial environment. Hopefully I would go to a firm that encouraged and supported young associate lawyers who wanted to spend time getting business and building their network. The firm was indeed known for being entrepreneurial even though it was good-sized. The partners all worked hard to develop business and had compensation structures that encouraged this.

The partners I spent time with in interviews were very clear that if I came there, not only would I join a culture that encourages all attorneys to develop new business, but I would be paid a percentage of the business I brought in (as all associates were). They said they would be happy to meet with me regularly to talk about my marketing strategy and would go out of their way to be available if I needed them to help me pitch a potential client. Of course, they said, they also needed me to work hard on projects for the firm and earn my salary, and I certainly understood that.

It seemed like a perfect match. I had two other offers at the same time (it was a good time in the economy and Wall Street—in other words, a long time ago!). One offer was from a smaller firm that was just getting started and only had about 10 lawyers, so I was concerned about joining something so small. Ironically, that firm now has 75 lawyers and has done very well.

My third offer was from a new firm breaking off from another with about 100 lawyers, but there my compensation would be a straight salary and maybe a bonus. Not what I was looking for if I was hoping (as I was) to bring in business. So I chose the entrepreneurial firm.

Almost immediately after my arrival the truth became clear. Two of their promises were true: I would receive a percentage of money I brought in, and I would be working on their projects. It wasn't a sweatshop, mind you, but it was a very hardworking place. I realized quickly that the only part of my bringing business that they would be happy about would be when a check arrived from one of the small handful of clients I developed there. Going out to get business, or even spending my time servicing it, was not looked on favorably by partners who only wanted to know if their work assigned to me was getting done (fyi none of the then partners in question remain in this firm(s)).

In one annual review I was told that, even though I was billing pretty much the same amount of hours as other associates, the perception was that I was constantly on the phone with my contacts trying to get business. Not long after that I finally decided that I had to break off and start my own firm. It took several years from that point to pull it off, but I knew then that it had to be done.

The mistake the firm partners made was saying what they felt they needed to in order to get me in the door even though the promises were, frankly, hollow. It guaranteed my stay there would not be long and that I would spend a good part of it resentful for arriving to see that things would not be as I hoped. In fairness, there were a few partners who tried to be supportive of my efforts to build a practice at a young age, but most were not.

As a result of this experience, I am always up-front with my potential hires about what I will expect from them and what they can expect in working with me.

Howard Stern Redux: Home Growing the Staff

We return once again to my business deity, Howard Stern. Howard does have an amazing ability to retain people on his team for many, many years. But how does he get them to join in the first place?

I describe Howard's current business as on a wonderful tear and frenzied. In addition to his radio show he is traveling the country judging *America's Got Talent*. He is also overseeing two 24-hours-a-day channels on Sirius/XM. But his business has been on a wonderful tear for most of 30 years. He has been playing some of his old radio shows recently, and I listened to one from his days as the morning man in Washington, D.C., in June 1982. Even then he was clearly funny and edgy; his sidekick, Robin Quivers, the dutiful foil; and sound effects guy, Fred Norris, bringing his own brand of humor.

For most of these 30 years, Howard was a celebrity, and presumably there was no shortage of folks desperately trying to work with him. But were they right for the show? Very early in his career he came upon Quivers, Norris, and his producer, Gary Dell'Abate (the famous "baba booey," whose nickname Stern fans scream in the background when heckling a live TV news shoot).

There were a few well-known hires that ultimately didn't work out: funny man Jackie "the joke man" Martling and comic Artie Lange. Martling did, however, stay for many years and added tremendous value to the show before an apparent salary dispute led to his departure. He has since returned not to the Stern show, but with his own weekly show on one of Stern's channels.

Artie Lange is a horribly sad story of depression, drug abuse, and ultimately a failed suicide attempt that finally removed him from the show. He is thankfully doing better and has his own Internet radio show now with a partner. And some of his best shows with Howard, frankly, were probably when he was high as a kite, very funny, a little over the top at times, but extremely talented. Artie also lasted nine years on the show, and it also took quite a bit of comfort-building with Howard before Artie permanently took over Martling's chair.

Howard has a knack for finding people to work with him who get the job done, love the excitement, put in long hours, are tremendously loyal, and have developed a real family, dysfunctional though it may be at times. You can't always tell which on-air fights between staffers or with Howard are real or kind of staged for the show, but it doesn't even matter. In the end, they all stay.

What is his secret? He often takes a long time to get to know potential employees through some other involvement with the show before thinking about bringing them on board. Some were longtime unpaid or barely paid interns before having a paid job. Others were regular contributors of material who eventually got coveted air time and developed a persona all before being added as characters to the program.

Another great hire was his longtime limo driver, who enhanced his position and became an on-air character himself, now running big "block parties" on weekends all over the country. But the driver, Ronnie Mund, was simply a reliable outsourced chauffeur for a long time before Howard made him a regular on-air contributor and his head of security.

Entrepreneurs don't always have the luxury of spending months or years getting to know potential hires. But keep in mind the possibility of future employment when you work with people who are employed by outside consultants, vendors, suppliers, customers, and, yes, competitors. You often get to know folks in these relationships, and can build a high level of trust and comfort before making a hiring decision.

While growth often requires mid-level hires that cannot be home grown, I have found that making an effort to build people from the bottom up often pays off. One of my most talented colleagues first worked for me as a paralegal while in college for three years part-time (full-time in the summers), then worked part-time all through law school, and by the time she arrived as a newly minted lawyer could hit the ground running rapidly and was almost immediately the equivalent of someone with at least one year's experience as an attorney.

Now as a fifth-year lawyer she is running transactions, supervising other attorneys, and, most importantly, great at her job in part because she was trained by me. That, to me, is a critical benefit of home growing your staff. When I hire laterally, while there are certainly exceptions, too often people come with bad habits that are difficult, if not impossible, to break. As I have said earlier, I try to macromanage and not cramp people's style, but bad habits can impede getting things done or lead to customer dissatisfaction.

So planning to focus on hires at a lower level and spending time making those hires is great for the long-term benefit of your growing enterprise. Just make sure you or someone very capable is prepared to spend the time to show the new employee the ropes. It will not always pay off, but if you select right, it will often enough.

Looking Inward and Building a Family

Is every entrepreneurial venture pretty much the same with regard to what types of employees are best for the company? Obviously not. So much depends on you, your needs, your personality, and the nature of your business. As you contemplate each hire, ask yourself some important questions: Am I more of a macromanager seeking employees who can take charge and confidently move proactively through projects with minimal supervision? Am I more of a control type with a plan to have more imple-menters whom I will guide rather intently? Will this employee interface with important relationships such as customers, vendors, and suppliers?

You need to be honest with yourself to get the right hires. A strong, independent employee will resist a micromanager. A less-confident employee will be nervous if left without much supervision. In some positions a warm and outgoing personality is critical; in others technical skill may be more important. Of course, the more senior the employee or executive, the more important these issues become, especially if the new employee will report directly to you.

And as you look inward, remember you are shaping a family with each new employee hire. So you need to make sure that your employees really do enjoy the adrenaline rush that comes with a fast-growing venture, maybe even with a big payoff for everyone someday. Think of all the Google sec-retaries who stuck it out and were well rewarded when the company went public; they're now millionaires!

As you build the family, hopefully you bring in folks who will like each other, enjoy working together, put the team ahead of their individual agendas (that's a hard one), avoid watching the clock, and plan for a long stay. Try to actually include that in your thoughts as you interview people. Get a sense of how outgoing they are and how much they could be real team players.

In making all hires, especially for more important positions, I worry. I worry that the person is really thinking of being with us just until his or her "real" dream opportunity comes along. For example, a talented young lawyer may be joining our firm in a tight job market but really wants to be in a larger firm and will leave as soon as he or she gets the chance. Some think if you can get a few years out of someone it's a worthwhile hire. I think differently. I make each hire hoping and believing that there is a real chance that this person will remain long-term.

To scope this out in the interview process, I ask the question outright: What's your long-term plan? Some actually think it's okay to say that long-term they hope to do something that is not working in my shop. I'd like to be a judge one day, someone told me. Another said she hoped to become an in-house lawyer for a big corporation one day. The smart ones say that they are thrilled to have this opportunity and think the boutique firm environment is exactly what they are looking for, and they would love it if it worked out so that this can be their long-term or even permanent home.

Then, when they say that, I have to assess whether I believe they are being truthful or just telling me what they think I want to hear. This is not easy to do, and I have not always read the answer correctly. One trick: Try a follow-up question, like "Why do you think this could be your long-term home?" See what that elicits. But bottom line: I am less likely to hire someone whose long-term plan has nothing to do with me or my firm. That may not be fair or realistic, but it has led to my bringing aboard key hires over the years who have stayed with me for a long time.

I would venture to say that major corporations are less focused on these types of attributes in their hires. About all that's really important there is: Can they do the job? Will they not embarrass themselves or the company? Is their resume strong enough so that the person making the hiring decision cannot be blamed if the person does not work out? That's really the difference: hiring based on the company's real needs, as opposed to just doing it right enough to make sure to cover your you-know-what.

I represent a small service business with about a dozen employees, one of whom had joined about a year earlier. Let's call him Bob. He was not perfect but did solid work and put in the appropriate number of hours. His resume was impressive, but his intelligence was a bit overshadowed by his lack of common sense and overwhelming shyness. He didn't even say hello to people in the morning—just quietly walked into his office, started typing, and didn't stop until the end of the day.

Bob was taken out in groups for lunch and drinks by the boss and would literally say nothing. Even if questions were asked of him, he would answer briefly and in a low tone that often required the questioner to ask him to repeat himself. After a year, Bob came into the boss's office and asked for a raise. In turn, the boss consulted with several key colleagues and decided to let Bob go.

Is that fair? In an entrepreneurial environment, unfortunately the answer may be yes. People who basically get their work done but are a negative life force in the glue that keeps the family together can hurt the entire company's work atmosphere. The boss decided that he could have another chance to hire someone who fits in more and at a lower salary. This he did a month later, and the new hire worked out great.

Issues Female Entrepreneurs Face in Hiring

Reality: For millions of years, until about 40 years ago, men ruled stuff. The world, business, all sources of power. Men were the hunters; women were the gatherers. Women had influence over their men, but men were, as former President George W. Bush might say, the deciders. Men worked outside the home, and women's job was to take care of the home and children. Women did not even have the right to vote in the United States until 1920.

The genders had their roles. I recall as a child in the 1960s my mother and sisters getting up from the dinner table to clear the dishes while my father and I sat. But when it snowed, I was the one who got up at 6 AM to shovel (okay, we did have a snow blower). These days our roles are more muddled. When I told a male friend this story he said, "Yeah, now we have to clear the table *and* shovel the snow."

The perception among some men that the old ways were better is not dead. When I first started my solo practice, I rented an office in a larger suite controlled by another company. I hired a high school intern for the summer who was attractive and typically well-dressed. One day she came to me and said that one of the other company's employees was making her uncomfortable. Whenever she stood up from her desk, she said, this employee would rush to his doorway and watch her walk out. He never said anything or touched her, but his behavior was clearly inappropriate.

I learned that as an employer I am responsible for the work environment even if the trouble comes from someone else's employee. (Keep this in mind if you are in a space-sharing situation.) So I went to the boss of the other company and told him the story. His first reaction: "I wouldn't let my 17-year-old leave the house dressed like that." I said that I frankly didn't think she dressed inappropriately and, more importantly, the guy we were talking about was the professional and should know better.

Then this silver-haired executive in his mid-50s said, "You know, my father was right. Women should not be in the workplace. All they do is distract us. My father had a male secretary for years and I think that was better." Of course I said what I always say in these situations: that in many ways women bring more to the table than the men, and make awesome contributions to business and society—but again, not the point as this guy was acting inappropriately.

He finally agreed to talk to his employee, and things got better after that. Shocking as it is, this attitude is still out there.

The way this manifests for a female entrepreneur in hiring decisions is multifold. One benefit for women starting their own business is to get away from dealing with harassment from bosses. But as women become bosses and business owners, they face the possibility of hiring men who might resent working for a woman. They face the risk that a man might not provide the appropriate respect for a female boss. One would hope to hire men who are gender-neutral in their views on who their boss should be, but the reality is that not all men are.

Women hiring women also has its challenges. It is said that some women resent working for other women, or they might be jealous that another woman has greater success than they do. While many women appreciate having female mentors to help them navigate some of the challenges we have been describing, the mentors (read: you as female entrepreneur) sometimes worry about the mentee overtaking their success.

So if it is a challenge for female entrepreneurs to hire men, and it is a challenge to hire women, what is there to do? Robot employees have not quite been perfected yet, so you have to pick one or the other. (I'm kidding.) And as we know, one cannot legally make a hiring decision based on gender.

Since I am not a woman, I am not the best advisor to female entrepreneurs on these issues. But I do think I know how men think, and what men say, and for that matter what women say, about working for a female. The simple answer: Some are fine with it and some are not.

The key, I think, in the hiring process is not ignoring the issue. Do your best to elicit what likelihood there may be that this potential employee will have an issue working for a woman. There is nothing wrong, for example, in asking if the person has ever worked for a woman and what that experience was like for him or her—not in a defensive way but with honesty and concern about an issue not discussed or addressed nearly enough.

Body language also can tell a lot in an interview. Is a male candidate being sort of flirty, or borderline condescending (both problems)? Is a female candidate leaning back with arms crossed (problem)? Is a male willing to give you a firm handshake (good sign)? Is a male having trouble with eye contact or are his eyes drifting in, um, the wrong places? Those all could be signs of an issue.

Bottom line: Address the issue up-front. You are more likely to make the right hire. Let's turn now to how to keep those fabulous employees you have so carefully hired.

Retaining Great Employees in Entrepreneurial Companies

As you see, it is hard enough to make the right selection up-front. What's even harder is keeping employees around, assuming you want that. Clearly the first decision in working on employee retention is figuring out whom you would like to retain. This does not mean that you must terminate each employee that you determine is not worth retaining. There are marginal employees who you may keep around for the time being, but if these people were to leave it would not harm the business and the individuals are replaceable.

So the focus on retention is on your top and strong performers who are doing a great job and would be more difficult to replace. These are the folks with whom you hope to spend years as your business family works together to build the company to the sky—people who will care about the business's success (and your success being tied to theirs), and who will give 150 percent all the time with a positive attitude and have none of the negative issues we have talked about in this chapter.

Friends of mine who have been in business many years often lament that the workers of today are not as dedicated as they were coming up. They believe that there is a sense of entitlement that focuses more on what's in it for them with the least amount of effort, as opposed to feeling pride in the work and commitment you put in for the benefit of the entire company. Do my friends have a warped sense of their own salad days? Maybe, but I have also encountered quite a bit of what they are describing.

Decades ago in law firms, it was pretty much understood that whatever firm you landed at after school was the firm where you would probably remain for your entire career. Rarely were lateral hires made mid-career. These days it is assumed and totally acceptable if young lawyers in big firms move to two to three different firms before making partner somewhere roughly 10 years after graduation.

Law firm partner mobility is less common than for associates, but there is lots of lateral partner movement these days. Many larger firms have attractive pension arrangements that encourage partner retention, but a large signing bonus for big rainmakers often solves that. What happened to loyalty? Let's explore that.

To Get Loyalty, Give Loyalty

Many employers expect loyalty from their employees. That no one would intentionally do something to hurt the business and that they will blindly follow the boss into all the craziness that an entrepreneurial environment creates. With loyalty also comes respect. I am to be respected as the boss, they think.

An entrepreneur client of mine had a dozen employees who were all hardworking. Frankly, he didn't really care much about them or their lives, was demanding on them work-wise, and was traveling the globe promoting the sale of his products and getting them manufactured. He would express to me his frustration at not keeping good people and really had no clue why the business was such a revolving door of employees. He tried to blame it on what he perceived as today's disappointing work ethic, suggesting that employees these days just don't have what it takes to be hard workers.

One of his senior executives finally confided in me, as he himself was getting ready to quit, that the staff really disliked the boss. His mistreatment and disregard for them, while also expecting gargantuan hours, bred resentment and frustration. One quit after the boss wouldn't let him attend the funeral of a longtime close friend. While their overall compensation was competitive, everything else about the work environment caused unhappiness. Put simply, they never felt the boss was there for them.

After the senior executive who told me about this left, I sat down with the client and talked about his management style and what I was hearing from his employees. He was flabbergasted, claimed to have no idea he was so difficult to work for, and said he was so focused on building and maintaining the business that thinking about the employees' happiness was not on his radar.

He actually hired a coach to work with him after this discussion and has since worked harder on employee retention. He has learned that respect and loyalty are not automatic, that they must be earned, and that it is critical for management to pay attention to those things that will lead to employee job satisfaction.

How do you do that in a crazy entrepreneurial environment? I think most people who have worked for me over the years as I built my law practice think I am a good boss, and I believe most have also respected my experience, my abilities, and my judgment. I have paid attention to giving respect and loyalty to my employees before expecting anything back. Here are some easy things to do.

One adage I have: It's nice to be nice. One of the least expensive ways to build employee loyalty is simply to be nice to them. You can do this while also being clear about your expectations and even clear when you are disappointed in their performance. Being mean or rude to employees never works. Yelling at people is rarely effective. Management by fear may yield a form of compliance, but it will not build loyalty or respect, which I believe are critical to obtain the best performance and productivity from employees.

Being nice also includes caring about their lives. I'm a naturally friendly person and, while not looking to interfere in the lives of my employees or cross a line from employer to friend (with a few exceptions), I want them to know that I care about what is happening in their lives outside of work. I try to take people to lunch occasionally, where I talk as little about work as possible.

I have also tried hard to arrange special events for the staff to relax away from the office together. Whether it's a traditional holiday party or a summer cocktail gathering, these are worthwhile bonding experiences for the team. It's also a nice way to let them know how much you appreciate how hard they work.

Being nice can be hard when you are having a rough day. There are times over the years that my office manager would see me and ask if something is wrong in the business. I would ask why she was asking.

Her response: You seem really down and distracted today. What she didn't know was that I may have had some issue completely unrelated to work that was troubling me, but I made the mistake of appearing worried or upset. Remember that, whether you realize it or not, the staff is watching you and taking their cues from you and your mood.

So do your best to compartmentalize your personal and business lives as much as you can. In addition, often the most important time to remain positive and friendly is when things are more challenging in the business. You may not want the staff to know if there is a serious problem until you are ready to explain it to them properly (like after you fix the problem). So at times you may be stuck in an acting role, playing the affable boss when things are going wrong. But, as we discussed in Chapter 2, always being the cheerleader is important to do, or the staff gets worried because you're worried, and the next thing that may happen is they are out the door.

Another great way to build loyalty is simply to listen. It's actually one of the harder things for a busy entrepreneur to do, but take the time to pay attention to ideas or thoughts that your team brings to you. And create an environment that encourages this opportunity. Make sure they know your door (or e-mail, if you prefer) is always open for suggestions and thoughts about how to do things better or improve the business. And then get back to them, make sure they know you thought about the suggestion, and provide a thoughtful and constructive response.

Helping staff when they are dealing with difficulties in their lives is also a critical part of building loyalty from employees. Remember my client who wouldn't let his employee go to a good friend's funeral? I had a longtime employee who lost his mother. I know how close he was to her, though I had never met her. In addition, his sister had worked for me for a number of years but had moved away. I knew she was coming for the funeral and just knew immediately that I should take the morning and go to Brooklyn for the wake. Do I do this every time? No. In the right circumstances, however, and with the right employee, your gut tells you the right thing to do. My employee was incredibly appreciative that I took the time to come.

Another key employee's father was ill and a plane ride away. It appeared her father was not going to make it. Our business was small enough that federal leave rules did not apply. But not only did I encourage the employee to go, I encouraged her to stay there as long as needed (within reason) and not have it count as vacation. She ended up out about a week and a half dealing with his passing and funeral, and was so thankful for our flexibility that she volunteered to come in on successive Saturdays to make up the time. I told her not to worry about it. Do I do this every time? No.

A number of businesses I know adjust their work hours in the summer, working four days a week for 10 hours a day. I am told by employers who do this that it creates tremendous goodwill and is greatly appreciated, although the staff is still putting in a full work week. Not every business can do this if there are too many things that can come up on a Friday. If you can, it might be something to consider.

Silly things like allowing the staff to wear jeans on Fridays actually go a long way to improving employee morale. Of course, again, it has to work with the particular business you are in. Once in a while I just surprise everyone and bring in a pizza party for lunch. Most years we made sure to celebrate every employee's birthday (my firm had gotten big enough at one point we had to just do it monthly for all the people whose birthdays fell in that month). Little things go a long way.

The risk with being too nice, of course, is that you are taken advantage of. "We can do X and the boss will never get mad" may be something you don't want to overhear if X is something you would rather they not do. There are those for whom sick days are really just extra personal days. Some employees having particularly rowdy weekends may enjoy a little "Monday flu," as I like to call it. If employees occasionally request to work from home because of some personal issue, that's fine, but if they are doing it just to get a partial day off, then of course that is a problem.

The answer is to deal with this employee by employee. When you show loyalty and respect, and feel you are getting them in return, you can be even stronger in that support. When you are not sure, well, maybe they move into that category of marginal worker whom the business can live without if they were to leave.

These approaches do not generally involve financial cost to the business, but failing to treat people right can result in losses in productivity and an unhappy work environment. Of course, there are ways to build loyalty that involve spending money. The "best companies to work for" typically offer such goodies as free or subsidized daycare, comfortable lounge areas with ping pong and video games to take breaks, free food and drink, a workout facility, trips to reward successful projects, onsite massages, flexible work hours, telecommuting, and the like.

Our law firm recently moved to permanent space in the iconic Chrysler Building in Manhattan after a stint in a shared office space. The addition of free snacks and soda in our new lunch room (along with coffee and water we always had) was greeted with a surprisingly large amount of enthusiasm.

Most growing companies do not have much excess cash for these benefits. If you can, great, but otherwise as noted previously there is much you can do that does not involve depleting the corporate treasury.

Another part of showing loyalty is to provide the proper compensation to each employee.

Structuring Compensation Right

There is the way normal businesses choose to put together employee compensation, and then there are entrepreneurial companies, where things can get a bit more complicated. You may think you know what will be the best motivator for an employee, but do you? Everyone just wants as much money as they can get as soon as they can get it, right?

That may be true, but some might be willing to sacrifice a little today to get a lot tomorrow, which of course is the whole point of the entrepreneurial adventure. But how do you know what compensation structure is right for your employees?

As with loyalty and going out of your way, the marginal employees whom you can take or leave typically require less attention when it comes to compensation. This initially seems harsh since each of these people is a human with bills to pay and maybe even a family to support. Should you care about that? Some say yes, that this is another benefit of starting your own business—to add a caring element to the tough business world and do more for those who need more even if their job performance may be only so-so. Truthfully this attitude is more common among female entrepreneurs.

Others say business is business and what initially seems harsh is actually in the best interest of the employee who is only okay, because it is letting them know that they are not achieving the best that you would like to see out of someone. Or you are letting them know that even trying their best is not good enough because their talents or abilities are limited. And we should not coddle people; they should face their limitations and adjust their expectations accordingly.

It really is all about attitude. If the marginal employee is putting in tremendous effort with a determined and focused approach, but just not cutting it, I will go out of my way to give him or her the benefit of the doubt until he or she becomes more of a liability than an asset. A well-intentioned person making a lot of mistakes is a problem. A well-intentioned person who is basically capable, but just not evolving and improving can sometimes be tolerated. Even then, these are not usually people who are key to your company's success.

So when it comes to ensuring that the employees who are important to your entrepreneurial company's future have a compensation arrangement that provides the most incentive for them to perform at their highest level with the greatest amount of personal satisfaction and loyalty, I tend to focus on two major factors. The first is balancing current versus future benefit. This is not always a simple task. How can you read someone's mind to determine what they might prefer?

Before answering this, let's be more specific about potential arrangements you may make. In addition to a normal salary, some prefer a commission-based arrangement. Others are happy with a salary and bonus that is either predetermined based on their performance or discretionary. But it is also very common for employees of growing companies to see some benefit if the company is sold down the road, or goes public, or is able to achieve some other liquidity event like a large dividend payment to equity owners.

Employees obtain that benefit most commonly through stock ownership in a company. But as we will discuss later in talking about partners, it is not always necessary to make employees stockholders for them to get the chance at that brass ring. Stock options are also a possibility. This allows you to retain control and not have obligations that accrue when you have fellow stockholders. The options can be exercisable upon a liquidity event but not before. And the options can be exercised either at a nominal price, or a more "real" price that either requires them to put up cash or exchange some "in the money" options as the exercise price for others, a so-called "cashless" exercise.

Another possibility is so-called "phantom stock." In this arrangement you have an agreement with employees that says that while they do not own stock, they will receive compensation as if they did if there is a liquidity moment like going public, sale, or a dividend. This way they avoid the need to exercise an option, they are not stockholders, and it is easily terminable if they leave the company.

Some have more simplified profit-sharing arrangements that are intended to provide incentives for the employees to maximize the company's current performance. And some combine a number of these approaches.

There are other potential structures, but the book isn't long enough! And of course these same structures can be applied whether the company is set up as a corporation, limited liability company, or even partnership. While this is not meant to be a legal book, realize there are legal complexities (especially tax-related) to these arrangements that need to be carefully worked out with your advisors.

The main thing to ask, however, to paraphrase the great movie *Field of Dreams*, is this: If you build it, will they care? If, for example, you tell employees being offered stock options in lieu of part of their compensation that your plan is to sell the company in five to seven years, how many will really appreciate that as a positive addition to their compensation package?

Some indeed may, if they are true believers in the potential of the company, plan on a long stay with you, and can handle the current financial reduction. Others may focus more on the food they must put on the table for their families, maybe are not so sure they plan to remain with you that long, or even frankly aren't feeling as sanguine as you about the business's potential.

Others simply are more risk-averse than others. You hired them, hopefully, in part because they will enjoy the exciting ride that is a fast-growing enterprise, but that doesn't mean they are ready to give up much current income in exchange for uncertain potential upside.

A client had a plan to sell his business within one to two years. He offered a dozen of his 50 employees stock options that they could only exercise if the company was sold, but he made clear that was his immediate plan. Darned if the company's performance didn't improve dramatically almost immediately, resulting in a higher-than-expected sale price of about $15 million just 18 months later. My client's longtime assistant walked away with a cool $200,000, and several key executives made over $1 million. It was worth it because without the improved performance my client estimates he might have sold for more like $8-10 million.

So how do you determine what will be the best motivator for each employee? One simple way is to offer them both alternatives: straight cash today, or less cash today and an opportunity for equity ownership or its equivalent. Maybe for every dollar less of salary they get $3 in today's value of stock, or something like that. See what they say. Again, in most companies this is limited to higher-level valuable employees, but I have seen others that, like Google and Microsoft, gave stock options to pretty much everyone before they went public.

Another method is to simply sit down with each employee and talk about what would make them feel the most incentivized to perform at their very highest level. You may well be surprised to hear the answers.

Remember that giving people equity may mean giving them the chance to see the company's financial performance. That is the advantage of options or phantom stock, which will not necessarily give them the right to see financial information. In some types of businesses, like family businesses, this may not be able to work. There may be things on the books that the family would rather not share with the employees.

In these cases, other incentives need to be found, like tying part of an employee's performance to their specific sales numbers or even the results of a profit center they may control, or providing that in the event of a sale an employee is guaranteed X months of pay as a sale bonus. In both of these cases, the staff would not need to see the company's books.

Finally, remember in structuring compensation to pay what in big law firm life we used to call "the going rate." What is the going rate, you ask? Just enough to keep you from going. It is not necessary to beat what your competitor is paying just because. You just need to pay enough so that an employee will not leave because of his or her compensation arrangement. This is not to suggest to undercut salaries, or to not be fair and competitive. It simply means to pay just enough so that an employee is indeed willing to accept what you are offering and then give 150 percent effort for the company.

This includes ensuring that you provide a proper benefits package to make people feel comfortable. It is not expensive to let people put away money in a 401(k) even if you don't match, but people appreciate it. If you can offer health insurance, people appreciate it.

Therefore . . .

Study after study show that being happy with the work environment, not just salary, is extremely important to workers. Of course compensation is also critical. To make sure your employees are indeed happy, as we have said, realize that it is important to make attracting and retaining the right talent a priority in your growing company. Doing this right requires time and the intelligent probing of candidates to make sure they not only have the necessary skills, but also the right personality and attitude to get along well with others.

Working at keeping people is equally—maybe even more—important. You must give loyalty to get it, be nice, and make sure your compensation is structured to make it the most likely that you will get the greatest performance out of your amazing hires.

CHAPTER 6

Finding the Right Business Partner for Your Venture

This chapter focuses on finding the right business partners (if any) to help build your dream. These partners, who own part of the business, tend to fall into one of four categories: founding partners, investor partners, rainmaking partners, or worker bee partners. We will explore each.

Before you decide to add partners, you should ask yourself a few questions. One assumes you left or are leaving your job to have the freedom to pursue your dream—your way—and you can't wait to be free from bosses and others telling you what to do. Are you ready, therefore, to have at least one other individual to whom you are accountable? Who may have joint decision making authority with you? With whom you may argue and disagree?

Or maybe it will be someone who will beautifully complement your skills and abilities, and take on aspects of the business that are either uninteresting to you or would not be your areas of strength. And someone with whom you will enjoy sharing both the successes and challenges of building a business.

The thing to remember: It is critical that you and any partner you decide to bring in are able to function together and get along.

A general rule of thumb with any potential partner is that if there are meaningful difficulties in making arrangements to become partners, there is a much greater likelihood that there will be major problems down the road. If the initial agreement process goes very smoothly, while that doesn't guarantee anything, my experience is you have a much better shot at a successful, happy partnership.

81

The downside of a bad partnership, of course, is that "corporate divorce" can be extremely nasty. Lawsuits can go on for years, cost dearly, and in too many cases cause the end of a promising business. In other cases, people try to stay together through the hard times, but the negative energy permeates the organization, creating "tribes" tied to one partner or the other, and significantly hurts the business.

Of course, amazing partnerships can help companies fly to the sky. Spreading the challenge of leadership successfully can help leverage opportunities, create efficiencies, and provide each other with critical moral support. Some just would rather not feel all alone in running a company.

But don't bring a partner in solely to assuage your fear of not sharing the load. I represented a young entrepreneur who ended up bringing in a much older partner solely because the partner promised a $25,000 equity investment in the startup, for which he received a 45 percent interest in the company. It turned out the partner was overly controlling, a bit emasculating, and condescending, and he used his money as a source of power. Too quickly, my client realized he could have managed without the $25,000 investment, and he seemed stuck with the investor. Luckily over a period of time some calm negotiations led to an amicable buyout of the partner, who made a tidy profit on his $25,000. But it doesn't always end this way.

Many entrepreneurs, however, do choose to go it alone—whether intentionally or not. Before diving into the different kinds of partners and the advantages and disadvantages of each, as well as the tricks and traps to avoid in these cases, first ask yourself if entrepreneurship may be better for you as a one-person show.

Do You Want to Fly Solo?

It is the ultimate entrepreneur's dream, no? Leaving the corporate world for an environment that is 100 percent in your control and in which 100 percent of the benefit of your hard work goes to you. Why would you want to share that with anyone if you don't have to? The answer, of course, is that you don't have to.

Many entrepreneurs indeed get started on their own. Others have an initial venture with partners, and then realize they are happier solo and look for ways to undo their relationship early on. We will talk more about that. There are, of course, both benefits and challenges when you plant your entrepreneurial flag all by yourself.

Although my initial foray into setting up my own law firm was with a partner (and ultimately three partners), after this I started a solo practice that, at least for the first six months, was literally just me. I then hired an associate and have not been all by myself since, although I remained the sole de facto owner of my law firm even when it grew to 40 employees.

But the six months alone was a unique experience. I used to think to myself, "I could take the afternoon off and go to the movies, and no one will care but me." That was an incredibly liberating thought. How many times did I go to the movies (and I love movies)? You know the answer.

But just knowing I had that freedom was wonderful. With partners, and even employees, you clearly have, or at least feel, a greater sense of responsibility to them. To me it didn't matter. Even alone, I had a responsibility to myself, and of course to my family, to work hard and do everything in my power to be successful.

Some people, however, realize that their desire to start something on their own is all about both independence and control, which do not always go together. For example, you may have an equal partner, but each of you trusts each other sufficiently to have the flexibility to go through your day and make many decisions without needing to check with each other. Hopefully you are on the same page often enough to avoid too many disagreements. So you may have less control but a great deal of independence.

In order to decide on solo versus partner(s), try to determine your willingness to share both control and independence. Some simply are not cut out to "play well with others," as they used to say on my elementary school report card. They need to be in charge and not be answerable to another. If not they can become frustrated, unhappy, and unmotivated, or worse, difficult, ornery, and belligerent.

In making my most recent move to combine my practice group with a larger firm I learned something about myself—namely, that I care much less about control than I do about independence. Luckily, the founders of our firm and I have a long history, and a great deal of mutual trust and respect. This means that I can work for the benefit of both the firm and building my practice pretty much as I see fit because they know that our mutual goals and priorities are the same.

It also means that I am comfortable with their control of decision making. This is because I trust they will make good decisions (which they have) and that they will consult with me on decisions that may affect me or where they believe my insight could be helpful (which they have).

But for many, control is indeed important. If that is the case, it may be a sign of an issue in your personality (read: the fictional Captain Queeg discussed in Chapter 2). But in many cases it can mean you are a natural leader who people are drawn to and who prefers the challenge along with the responsibility of taking charge. Some entrepreneurs are simply larger than life, and not only do they enjoy being "the decider," but their team looks to them for that very thing.

They say it is lonely at the top, but most solo entrepreneurs do not feel that way. One key to a successful one-person deal: make sure to have good advisers around you, who are not employees, to help keep you grounded and give you objective advice. Having strong legal and accounting advisers is a great way to start, especially if they have good experience working with early-stage and growing companies.

As you grow, you may find benefit in bringing in strategic or financial consultants. Others hire business coaches to help work on how you manage yourself and your people. And many are lucky enough to have great life partners, a spouse or significant other, who are solid sounding boards and ready to give you that jolt of reality that no one else can.

But for the rest of you, it's partner land. Let's dive into the different types of partners and how to best navigate sharing both successes and challenges with others.

Founding Partners

When you start a business with others, in a perfect world you decide up-front a number of things: how the pie is to be divided, what happens if one of you leaves, dies, or becomes disabled, how decisions will be made together, and so on. Unfortunately, the world is not perfect, and most co-founders do not initially start a business with a clear understanding of these items. Is this a good idea? Nope.

But let's step back just a bit. Assume you are indeed starting a business together with one or more potential partners. In most cases, there is really one person who is the primary driver of the idea, who brought the other partners in, etc. In that case, I strongly recommend making sure you really need this other person, because if things go as you hope, and the other person is replaceable, you will provide a significant windfall for the privilege.

A solo entrepreneur client decided to hand 40 percent of their early stage business to someone who will be providing needed technical assistance for this online retailing company. The rationale? This person's work is needed for the company to succeed and the company has no money to pay him. Plus my client believed the additional person would be a worthwhile long term addition to the team.

The client went ahead with the deal, but only after we got involved and suggested some protections, like making clear that my client remained majority owner and can make all decisions, and that my client would have the right to buy out the new partner's interest in the future, with some restrictions. Important lesson: It's way easier to get into things than out of them, so make sure you think about an exit strategy from a new relationship right up-front.

This client got the benefit of the partner's services without being tied to him forever, and potentially obtaining the equity back so as ultimately to return the maximum upside to the founder. This is not always possible, but in this case was agreed. Think of it as the business pre-nup.

Best friends, those who are romantically involved, or families that start a business together create other issues. The positive, of course, is the chance to spend so much time with people you care so much about and, also, presumably, people you respect from a business perspective.

Best Friend Partners

There are great stories about college roommates starting something cool in the dorm room that takes them past college to great acclaim. With a best friend, of course, is the risk that the friendship gets severely tested in the process of building the business, in much the same way that a romantic relationship gets tested in times of stress and adversity. Make sure that it is worth risking the friendship to build the business, and find ways to separate your business selves from your friend selves as much as possible.

I have one client company whose two female best friend owners make sure to go out for drinks with each other (sometimes with friends, sometimes not) at least once a week with a promise to discuss no business when they do. This can help.

Also realize it is always possible that something interferes with your friendship even though things may be fine in the business. Maybe one partner gets seriously involved with someone that the other partner dislikes, leading to a weakening of the friendship. While you deal with that as you would when there is no business between you, don't lose sight of the importance of maintaining a happy business relationship.

In reverse, of course, do your best to ensure that business problems do not hurt the friendship. Make sure you are respectful to each other at all times, even in times of disagreement or struggle. Try to make the struggle your joint struggle—the "shared misery" concept of my life in big law firms.

And you never know what can come of it. A male and female friend I know started a business. Both were romantically involved with others and just knew they'd make great business partners in a retail venture. They started doing well, spending enormous amounts of time together. About six months after they both lost their significant others, in part because of the demands of the business, he declared his love to her and they were married six months later. And yes, they are still happy business partners.

Couple Partners

If you are starting a business as a romantic couple, these issues become even more complicated. The most obvious question: What if you break up? Even if you are married, we know 50 percent of all marriages end in divorce. What happens to the business then? Also, how do you make sure that you are not talking business 24/7?

I used to represent a cool company started by a gay couple. It grew nicely for several years, and then they broke up romantically. Undaunted, they decided they still got along in running the business and continued together. Unfortunately, however, one partner lost interest and was not showing up as much, was constantly surfing the web when he was there, and was less and less valuable to the business.

There was an agreement between them, but it required a determination of "cause" before one partner could kick out the other. The partner who was still working hard attempted to terminate the other for cause. This led to a long legal battle and a rather expensive settlement. Thus, even where you have agreements that supposedly govern a situation, a nasty business breakup following a nasty romantic breakup can really ruin your day. Think long and hard before starting a business as a couple, or at least accept the fact that you will have a difficult time separating the private relationship from the business relationship.

However, I know many successful spousal business partners who have done a great job building businesses together. Good friends of mine have run a fashion business for over 10 years that has given them a nice lifestyle. He is the back office; she is the face to the outside world. His parents, who are also involved in the business, built their own businesses together successfully, creating great role models.

After getting the kids off to school, they take the train every day to and from Manhattan together. He helps pick up for her when she needs to stay home to deal with an issue with the kids, and he is Mr. Mom when she travels overseas for sales purposes. They've made it work, and for them, the benefits far outweigh the challenges.

Family Partners

And what of family businesses, which are seemingly so wholesome and American? I have represented many family businesses and close friends who represent the second or third generation of successful family ventures. Family businesses aren't immune to the risks every other business faces, and they come with a new set of risks as well.

The first risk in family business is that the match is made because of a blood connection that may not be a smart business connection. Usually one member of the family is more dominant, more intelligent, or more ambitious than others. That person will always feel like he or she unfairly bears the burden and is not properly compensated while other family "freeloaders" don't work as hard. Sometimes interests in the business are simply handed to non-working family members out of some sense of fairness. This leads to resentment.

Another risk is that a perceived positive is illusory—namely, that at least with family everyone can trust each other. Unfortunately, in too many situations family members cheat, steal, and backstab each other, sometimes because they are dealing with petty jealousies that go back to childhood.

In multi-generational situations these problems can be even more complex. When, if at all, does the older generation cede control to the youngsters? After five years? Ten? Twenty? Remember my client whose two sons came into the business and left because Dad was so controlling, only coming back when his mental state deteriorated? That is clearly not a situation anyone would have hoped for.

Another friend's family owns a distribution business in the Southeast United States. Two brothers started it, and eventually one died. The other had a son in the business and two daughters (not involved but owning part of the company). The problem was that the son in the business was not terribly motivated, was much happier in his non-business life, and never had any sense of ambition. As a result, the father never really pushed him to a senior position. Then the father died, and now, unfortunately the business has to be sold, as there are no other family members able to take over.

Yet I have another client where the second generation, having built the business to nine figures, told the younger group when they hit their late 30s that it was their turn. They said they would be heading South for the winter and to call if they're needed. Were they ready? Not clear, but they took over and knew they could always call on the elders when necessary, which they did often at first, and then less. This, you hope, is how the family business builds and succeeds.

Get an Attorney and Get It in Writing

In addition, it is indeed important when starting a business with others to have a clear understanding of what your business arrangement is between you. Even though you still may end up fighting about it later, it is better to have something in writing than not, if for no other reason than to go through the exercise of deciding how you want to run the business. Don't fall into the trap of saying, "Let's wait until something real is here and then we'll spend the few thousand dollars to put a proper agreement together." You're much less likely to ever get around to it, and if you do get around to it, your leverage and situation will be different after the business has moved forward a bit.

A typical arrangement for two people might work as follows: You agree that one of you is chairman and the other president and/or CEO. You are both board members. If one of you dies or becomes disabled, the other can buy his or her interest over time from the estate at a fair market value. If one of you simply walks out, there can be another buyout option, but this time at a discount to the fair market value to "punish" walking out. The same discount could apply if one of you has to make the other leave for cause. In both cases the discount from market value can diminish over time, since walking out after five years arguably should be punished less than walking out after six months.

Even if you are not equal partners, you may make a list of major decisions that can only be made jointly, or if the business is small enough, say that anything involving over $X has to be decided together. If one of you is putting in money and not the other, how to divide the pie has to be carefully done. Should the investor partner get his or her money out of profits first, before other money is distributed to the other? Does this partner just get a larger percentage of everything? Both? These are decisions that are unique to each situation.

And what if you reach a deadlock on an important decision? Some agreements call for a so-called "buy/sell" arrangement, which requires one partner to offer a price to either buy out the partner or be bought out, but the other partner decides which it will be. This theoretically leads to a fairer initial offer.

Others use "baseball arbitration." Here, much like in Major League Baseball, each side submits its best offer to an arbitrator and makes its arguments to defend it. The arbitrator has to pick one or the other offer—no compromise. Again, the idea is that each side will think hard about picking an outlandish number.

When you are ready to make these arrangements, it is important to make a small investment in both an attorney and accountant to help you structure the business properly. Web sites that allow you to form a corporation or LLC without an attorney's help are not sufficient. They don't tell you, for example, whether a corporation or LLC is better for you, or how to divide things up once you do get the entity formed.

I know a number of corporate attorneys who make favorable financial arrangements with new companies if they feel something promising may develop. Some will take equity as part payment, if you are willing to part with it (but remember again the possible windfall they will receive). Don't just find the lawyer with the cheapest base rate; the old adage "you get what you pay for" applies for real here.

There is a minor side question regarding lawyers—namely, whom the lawyer represents. Generally partners bring me in to represent the company in helping arrange the deal between partners, but then I do not represent either partner and am not there to protect either's individual interests, versus that of the business. I then recommend that each partner have his or her own attorney as well to review whatever documents I prepare.

Most partners ignore my advice because they are not able to bear the cost. When there are no other lawyers I do my best to help the partners wade through the issues and decide on how to resolve things in a fair way.

Investor Partners

Assuming you want or need and can find investors, they come in all different shapes and sizes. We will have much more on finding the right investor in the next chapter, but here our focus is on seeking the right "fit" in terms of your relationship with an investor partner. An investor partner, of course, is someone who provides needed capital to the business as a loan or in exchange for ownership in the business.

In addition to traditional bank loans and government financing from agencies such as the U.S. Small Business Administration, investors may be so-called "friends and family," angel investors, venture capital or private equity firms, or, if you are a public company, so called PIPE (private investment in public equity) investors, which tend to be hedge funds.

We'll cover three deciding factors in choosing the ideal investor. First is how much say you are willing to allow the investors to have. Second is how much ownership the investor will want in your company. Third is how much help and involvement with the company the investor will have. Let's examine each one.

Investor Veto Powers

If you are okay providing some decision making or veto power to your investor partner, then venture capital or private equity may be for you. They tend to put in what they call protective provisions, which include a list of important company decisions that cannot be made without their consent. Friends and family and PIPE investors do not typically require these veto powers. Some entrepreneurs actually like the idea that important decisions have to be run by an experienced professional investor; others resent it as interfering with their independence. One client lamented his frustration at his investor partner by telling me, "I already have a mom. I don't need another."

If you do go with venture capital or private equity, make sure you understand the documents. One client told me, "It wasn't until it was too late that I realized they could throw me out of my own company." And I have seen it happen. In a famous story about a well-known venture capitalist (VC) I know, he arrived at the headquarters or a company they had invested in, only to find a brand new big Mercedes in the founder/CEO's parking spot. He went inside and fired the guy on the spot, angered at this profligate spending. He later said many other things were leading him to that decision, and it wasn't just about the Mercedes. The point, however, is the VC had this power.

Settling on Valuation

Next, how do you decide what ownership to provide to an investor? Well actually, you don't decide; you and the investor decide together. Or rather, whoever has the most leverage tends to decide. How badly do you need this money, and how many potential sources do you have? If you need it badly and have no other sources, your investor will get what he wants. There's an old axiom on Wall Street called the golden rule: He who has the gold makes the rules.

Occasionally you are lucky enough to be a hot company and investors are competing to put money in. This is pretty rare, and only happens in frothy economic times and only to a select few companies. Even then, it's important to remember that there are other factors to consider beyond valuation, including the power the investor will have over you, as just described, and how involved the investor will be.

But back to value. There are probably 12 different legitimate ways to value a business. Public companies tend to be valued mostly on how their stock is trading, but not always. A valuation on a private company is often a combination of historical performance and future projected earnings. If you agree on a value of, say $5 million for your company before the investment (we call that the "pre-money value"), and an investor is putting in $1 million, then after the investment the company is worth $6 million (the "post-money value"), and therefore the $1 million buys one-sixth of the company because it is $1 million out of the $6 million post-money value.

All that is nice, but who gives you the most favorable valuation? In general that prize will go to friends and family. They are typically not professional investors and are investing at least in part with a bet on you or maybe even as sort of a personal favor, and are a little less interested in, say, a 10 percent better valuation. But professional investors, from angels to VCs to PIPE investors, do care about maximizing their ownership going in.

Watching hundreds of companies try to raise money over my career, one of the biggest mistakes I see entrepreneurs make in seeking capital is to overvalue their business. When investors are telling you your company is worth $10 million and you think it's worth $75 million, you are not going to raise that money—period. When you're arguing between $10 and $20 million, maybe middle ground can be found. But I've watched a number of companies crash and burn over this issue.

That brings us to another mistake to avoid. Back when I first started my independent practice, we also had a small venture capital firm looking to invest in early-stage companies. One company we were excited about made high-end, professional-style ovens and ranges for the home. We visited a number of times and were close to making an investment decision.

They gave us projections to cover the next three years that they strongly defended as conservative and achievable. We therefore suggested tying management's compensation primarily to achieving the projections, and even said they'd get the amounts they were seeking for themselves if they got to only 75 percent of the projections. When they refused to do that, we walked from the deal.

The lesson from that story is to only deliver projections that you really believe in so much that you would be willing to tie your compensation to achieving them. Of course, the challenge is not having such conservative projections that send an investor away because your plan does not include that much upside. But the infamous "hockey stick," fly-to-the-sky projections rarely sway investors positively.

Investor Involvement

How much do you want your new investor partner to be in your business face? Again, each entrepreneur is different. I have seen more than a few companies eschew venture-type financing because they did not want the collars, restrictions, and hovering that often accompanies that type of investment. Others understand the process and actually appreciate the help, assistance, and guidance that come from having an experienced investor and businessperson around.

The big question usually is whether the investor will have one or more seats on your board of directors. In general PIPE investors do not want to go on the board if you are public. That is in part because their ability to trade actively in the stock may be limited if they are around so much non-public information. Friends and family typically do not seek board involvement, but VCs, angels, and private equity sources usually do. Some even insist, after they invest, that the company hire their firm as a consultant for thousands of dollars a month.

Can this be bad? It can, sometimes. First, the whole "I'm starting a business and doing things my way" is basically out the window. You may disagree on important decisions. The board representative may be difficult and overbearing. Or worse, he or she may be totally disengaged since he or she is serving on 15 other boards.

In general, investors spend their most time on their portfolio companies that are doing the best and the worst. The ones in between simply don't get that much attention. And most investors will admit that they spend too much time on the "dogs," mostly out of pride and frustration in not wanting to let a bad company go. So you may need the board to spend some time and focus on something, and your investor representative is simply unavailable.

But as most investors will tell you, their involvement can also be tremendously helpful to a company. Good investors will help introduce you to important relationships such as banks, and accounting and legal firms, and help find manufacturing capability or even potential customers. They can also provide guidance in managing the business based on their years of overseeing many growing companies. More and more VC firms include partners who did not come out of finance, but rather out of operating businesses. So they "feel your pain" as they help you deal with challenges.

Always remember that almost every investor's number-one thought at all times is about the exit. When and how will the investor be able to monetize a solid return on his or her investment? Make sure going in that you have the same goals with the investor in that regard. If, for example, an investor is expecting a sale or other liquidity event like going public in two to four years but you would not like to do that for more like five to seven years, then you have a real problem.

Rainmaking Partners

If you have a key employee who is out producing revenue for the company—"making rain," as we call it—you may consider offering that person some ownership in the company. As with worker bee partners (which we will discuss), the real issue is making a policy decision to hoard or not hoard the equity in your business. Investors have to take equity, but employees do not. So first let's explore whether you should consider doing so with rainmakers, then talk about some of the different potential ways to grant ownership: direct stock grant, stock options, and phantom equity.

Determining the Need for Equity

Before offering ownership to a rainmaker, consider to what extent the grant will result in a meaningful incentive that will really motivate the executive even more than the rest of his or her compensation. There is no point in doing it if it is not likely to make a difference in his or her performance.

If your business is set up as a corporation, in most states someone with share ownership has legal rights, including the right to see the company's financial statements. He or she also has the right not to be "oppressed" as minority owners by the majority owners. This means the majority cannot take an action to benefit themselves at the expense of the minority. If you are an LLC or partnership, he or she would only have those rights typically if your LLC or partnership agreement says so. But again, make sure you are okay with the employee having some right to information and the right to some protection.

Also ask yourself if your employee will perceive that you are providing equity in place of some other aspect of compensation, and that they are okay with this. As discussed earlier, some employees care more about current compensation and paying their bills than a possible bigger payday down the road. Others want to be part of the ride. Those people enjoy being able to participate in the excitement of the possible slot machine payoff later on. Get a sense of which of these categories your employee fits into before offering equity.

In addition, to reiterate our earlier discussion, if you believe equity is a good idea and the employee is excited about the concept, make sure to offer something that will create real incentive. If you give someone stock but you don't plan to sell the company for 10 years, for most people that probably is not meaningful. Yes, for some just the prestige of being a "partner" is enough, but in most cases it is as much about the money.

In my case, the last law firm I created ran for 14 years with as many as 10 rainmakers and 40 employees, but I was the only one who owned equity in the firm. I called the rainmakers partners, but they were "contract" partners, with the title but no actual ownership. This worked for us for several reasons. First, the law business is unique in that you can't really sell a law firm. Firms merge all the time but rarely are big cash "buyout" payments made in those cases. So ownership for that reason has less real value.

Second, while the partners had no equity, I made a point of having strong communication ties with each. Any decision that might affect a partner was not made without getting his input and considering it. All major decisions, such as what healthcare plan to have or what level of staffing we needed, were brought to a monthly partner lunch, and everyone had a chance to weigh in.

There were many times that I changed my mind on something because my partners convinced me to, even though they had no legal say. Also, they had full access to the firm's financial records and received a daily "cash report" letting them know what monies had been received from clients each day.

Third, we all agreed that whether or not they had equity, what mattered to each of them was whether they were satisfied with their overall compensation. And each of them was, because we were structured with an "eat what you kill" arrangement. Partners did not receive a salary, only a percentage of the business they brought to the firm or serviced for another partner. Each ran a small entrepreneurial venture within our firm, but we provided administrative support, and each had the ability to "sell" a larger firm to potential clients.

Successful businesses *can* run without sharing equity. If you decide to do so, here are several approaches, expanding a bit on the brief overview in the last chapter. These can also be used with worker bee partners that we will discuss below.

Direct Stock Grants

In some cases companies simply hand stock (or other form of ownership interest) to key employees. Sometimes the ownership vests over time as an incentive to stick around. Sometimes the stock has to be returned if the employee leaves. Whether you have to buy out the shares or they are simply forfeited depends on the situation. Other times the company simply has an option to buy the shares back if someone leaves.

What can get complicated in a direct stock grant is tax. In some cases, the employee has to recognize the value of the stock as taxable income and pay tax on it. There are ways to sometimes delay this, but you need to make sure that the accountants review the tax impact if you are doing a direct stock grant. There are also tax-favored stock grants as part of an overall company plan that are possible.

The flip side of the employee taking it as income is the company getting to deduct the value of the shares for tax purposes. That's good if the company wants to reduce taxes, but can be bad, especially for a public company, because it makes earnings look lower.

The direct stock grant is most likely to give the most rights to the employee recipient, as we discussed. They may have the ability to see the company's financial statements, list of stockholders, and other key information. Some entrepreneurs simply do not want to share this information, in which case a desire to give ownership may have to take the form of an option or phantom equity.

Stock Options

Stock options are not only for public companies. Any company can give people options to acquire stock in the future at some specified price (the "exercise price"). In most cases, that price has to be equal to the value of the stock on the day you grant the option, but again, this needs input from accountants and tax folks, and is not the purview of this book.

Stock options are good because they reward an employee's effort to increase the value of the company, since the options are only "in the money" and valuable if the exercise price is below the value when you exercise. So if you give someone an option to buy stock at $5 and that is the value today, it is only worthwhile if you build the company to a point where the stock is worth more than $5. Otherwise there is no point in exercising and purchasing the stock, because when you go to sell the stock you would lose money or at least not make any.

Options are also good because, if structured right, there is no tax to the recipients when they get the option, or when they exercise and buy the stock. The only tax is when the stock is sold down the road. As with stock grants, you can vest options over time, and take them away if someone leaves. Here there's generally no buyout of the options if the employee leaves; they are simply canceled.

In private growing companies, it may be that you don't want to have to deal with employees as actual shareholders unless there's some major liquidity event like selling or going public. As I mentioned earlier, this worked for a client of mine planning a sale of his company within two years. He granted employees options but the only time the optionees could exercise and buy the stock was if the company was sold or went public. When he sold, they all exercised and had a very nice payday.

As mentioned in the last chapter, another feature you can add to stock options is so-called cashless exercise. Follow this: If you have an option to buy 100 shares of stock at $5 a share, and now the stock is worth $10, you allow the optionee to forfeit one half (50) of the options essentially as the exercise price for the other half. You can do this because the 50 shares forfeited have a net value (current stock price minus exercise price) of $5 a share, or $250, which is the exercise price needed for the other half.

The advantage of cashless exercise is that the employee does not have to lay out any money to exercise. The disadvantage is the employee has to give up a portion of his or her shares to do it. Also, some companies look at option exercises as an indirect way for the company to raise a little money, and this also goes away with cashless exercise.

Phantom Equity

As previously discussed, a neat alternative to stock or options is phantom equity. Here you simply sign an agreement that says if something happens that would benefit the stockholders financially, the employee gets some percentage of that as if he or she were an equity owner. It can go up or down over time, or be contingent on certain events, and can terminate if the employee leaves.

This is another approach that can have tax implications. If you do it correctly, after exercising a stock option or selling directly granted stock, you may be able to qualify for capital gains tax treatment on the eventual sale of the stock. As we know, capital gains tax is, as of the writing of this book, much lower than ordinary income tax that we pay on compensation.

Unfortunately, money received in a phantom equity arrangement cannot qualify for capital gains tax treatment. The recipient will have to report it as ordinary income and pay the higher tax. Again, the company gets a deduction, so in some cases companies offer a greater phantom equity reward to offset the tax benefit the company gets.

The key advantage of phantom equity is its flexibility. Yes, the benefit can vest as with the other methods. But you can add features like "unvesting" if certain negative things happen. It also never gives the grantee any direct or indirect ownership with the possible rights to information and protection that stock ownership can.

This approach is the least like ownership of the alternatives, so if the optics of being a "partner" are important, this might not be an ideal option. If it's all about the potential financial reward, phantom equity can be an effective method.

Worker Bee Partners

We've explored founding partners, investor partners, and rainmaking partners. And what of the lowly worker bee partners? Won't they happily slave away for a good salary and an occasional pat on the back? Actually, most entrepreneurs improperly downplay the importance of the folks who implement things, assuming incorrectly they are basically fungible and that rainmaking is more important. As discussed in the last chapter, getting and keeping good people is not easy. In truth, no one appreciates "a piece of the business" more than worker bees. And it is easier to negotiate terms, as they are likely to be thrilled just to be offered ownership.

Remember the challenges of bringing in the right types of employees we discussed. Hopefully you've worked hard to attract employees who will fit well into the entrepreneurial environment, including the excitement of a possible bigger payday down the road. It is for this reason that some clients of mine in private growing companies offer equity-type incentives for most if not all employees. The idea of "everyone is a partner" has a nice ring to it and hopefully bonds the employees even more to the company.

Of course, the right balance has to be struck. Rainmaker partners sometimes have compensation structures that are at least partially contingent on their efforts, so they are used to having a risk component to their arrangement and are more likely to appreciate the equity, even if it is in part in exchange for other compensation.

Worker bees are more likely to need the regular income to pay their bills and survive. You may need to consider the equity component as mostly in addition to their regular salary and not in replacement thereof. But the good news is that you don't necessarily have to offer that much equity to have a big impact. When a very helpful administrative assistant who makes $45,000 a year gets the equivalent of, say, $7,500 worth of stock, he or she may be absolutely thrilled; the rainmaker earning $100,000 a year might not appreciate that amount.

As with rainmakers, it is important to discern how much the worker bee will appreciate the equity. As your business grows it may not be possible to ensure that every new employee is excited about entrepreneurship. Some may simply need a job, and accept it out of necessity or some other reason you might never know. For these folks, equity might not be a strong motivator.

Of course the problem becomes when you offer equity to some but not others. Even if you do so for good reason based on performance or your perception of the likelihood it will indeed motivate them, everyone will talk to each other, and this could lead to resentment. Therefore, here's a good tip:

Either offer it in some form across the board, or set very clear guidelines so that the employees understand what qualifies someone for the equity piece.

One thing I have learned in my decades in business: When you ask employees to keep something to themselves, especially some kind of "special deal" you may be giving them over other employees, you have to assume, unfortunately, that the employees will do anything but keep it to themselves. I always like to say that everyone has one person they trust, even with "secret" information that he or she is not supposed to share with anyone. When employees tell their one person, then that person tells his or her one person, and so on until the word is out.

The other way information comes out is through leaks. Whether you like it or not, some lower-level employees have to find out about the company's compensation arrangements, unless you want to personally interface with your payroll company every month to send them your information. You hope you can trust them, but alas, it goes back to the "one person you trust" problem.

Leaks can also come from higher levels. A friend who leads a small architectural firm with six partners likes to talk about one of his young partners who regularly blabs to the employees about everything that is going on. Why does he do this? Who knows.

It was not that simple to figure out where leaks were coming from, but when the young partner was suspected, my friend gave him a false piece of information, saying the firm was about to double what employees have to contribute to health insurance premiums, and told no one else. When two days later five employees came into my friend's office to complain about "the rumor" they heard, he knew he had his man. The partner wasn't fired, but after his call to my friend's carpet and some pretty stern words, things improved.

In structuring equity offers to worker bees, I have seen a variety of structures, including phantom stock and stock options. With workers versus rainmakers, I have seen more arrangements for stock with no voting rights. Workers are less likely to feel they need a right to vote as long as they can participate in an eventual sale or IPO.

While Facebook isn't the greatest example, given all the challenges in its IPO, I love the story of the artist who was commissioned by the company to paint a mural on the wall of their first major office. The artist would have charged $60,000, but agreed to take stock with that value instead. When Facebook went public, his stock was worth $200 million! He also admitted that he had sold a large chunk of it privately before the company went public and the stock ended up much lower than its initial offering price.

Also important for both worker bees and rainmakers is to provide for a way to take back the equity granted if they leave the company. It is easier with workers to provide that the equity is simply forfeited rather than repurchased.

Therefore . . .

First, determine if you need a partner. If you do, plan your deal with them carefully and get it in writing. I'm going to say that again: Get it in writing! There have been too many disputes involving "he said, she said" allegations of who thought what deal was applicable. Determine your threshold for tolerance of what rights partners should have, and then think about whether your employees should also share in the pie.

Whenever you take in a partner, remember that you must run the business cleanly, without creating the "piggy bank" that entrepreneurial companies sometimes become for the founder. Because while you will always be the founder of the company you started, once you take on someone as any of these four types of partners, you are no longer truly its sole owner.

CHAPTER 7

Financing Your Company's Growth

The 6 Most Common Methods of Financing

This chapter focuses on how to navigate the challenging process of obtaining financing for your entrepreneurial company's growth. Financing is truly the trough at which growing businesses feed. Having been involved as a principal or attorney in literally hundreds of financings in my career, I can tell you that no two deals are alike.

Also, there is no perfect way to raise money. Each method comes with advantages and disadvantages, benefits and challenges. The key is finding the right match between a source of financing and your company's needs and culture.

Done right, a great match brings needed cash to fund the business's growth, and hopefully also a constructive and supportive partner who adds value to the team. Flip it around, of course, and a bad combination can result in acrimonious battles, harm to the business, and sometimes even the risk of losing your own company.

Here's a nice example from my world of reverse mergers: In 2006, Cougar Biotechnology, a relative start-up, merged with a shell company that was my client. At the same time they raised $50 million from institutional investors who had virtually no rights to direct the business. Within a year the company's stock was trading in a difficult environment. They then raised several hundred million dollars more. Luckily, the investors had limited ability to interfere with the company's business, which proceeded despite concerns about the market, and made good use of the money they had raised. Three years later, in 2009, the company was sold to Johnson & Johnson for nearly $1 billion.

I have another good example, albeit on a smaller scale. A client started a company from scratch in the computer industry. He used $20,000 of his own money to get going and built very slowly over the first few years, managing to sell just enough to keep his payroll going. Soon sales built more quickly and he generated enough profit to really grow the business, which hit $20 million in sales after 10 years and about $2.5 million in profit each year—a nice living! But he typically poured most of the profit back into the business to grow it even more. Finally at $25 million in sales and $3 million in profit, he decided to sell, which he did, for $18 million in cash to a much larger competitor. This was all done without outside financing.

A less-good outcome: I incorporated a new company in the apparel world. They immediately raised $1 million from individual investors, then a few years later went public and raised another $20 million. They depended heavily on accounts receivable financing to purchase goods, to the tune of about $25 million each year for a company that at its peak had $110 million in sales. When sales took a dip for two quarters in a row, the lender pulled the receivables financing line and the company went out of business because it could no longer acquire goods. This was all because they lost their financing.

Let's explore what affects the market for financing, then go through some basics of how deals progress, and finally dive into the six most common methods of raising money for an entrepreneurial venture.

Financing Market Drivers

In the end, the "golden rule" of finance governs if you need money to grow and have limited options. So all the discussion in here could easily be moot if you have one source of financing and your business will not grow without it. In that case, unless you are ready to give up the business, you will have to accept whatever terms are being offered and whatever powers the investor is seeking. Of course, hopefully you will bring in seasoned professionals (a-hem) to do the best they can to ensure that you are treated fairly overall.

In this section, we discuss what affects the market for financing, including the economy, stock markets, particular industry ebbs and flows, the regulatory environment, and even the presidential election cycle.

The Economy and Stock Market

The ability to raise money depends on the relative availability of that money. The more sources of financing exist, clearly, the greater likelihood of your accessing it. If you step back, that means that the more willing banks, and venture capital, angel, private equity, and individual investors are out there, the better. So what affects the "supply" of financing dollars?

Investor funds formed to do private equity or venture capital investments typically have a 10-year life. That means at any time there are funds whose lives are expiring. If the economy or stock market is down, it's a bit harder for the same venture or private equity fund managers to raise a new fund. And there are periods where many funds expire because a period 10 years earlier was frothier for fundraising. This creates more risk if that moment of expiration of many funds is not a great time for new fundraising.

In addition, even funds with cash to invest will, during certain periods, simply wait on the sidelines with respect to making new investments. Depending on their investment philosophy, some may love to jump in when the markets and economy are good even if that means paying a little bit more. Some have contrarian philosophies and invest only when things are looking bleaker. In general, as you might imagine, however, it is easier to raise money when the market and economy are strong versus the alternative (a little frustrating given my belief that the best time to start a new business is in the depths of a recession).

Even if you are an early-stage private company, often investors are looking at comparable public companies in making their investment decisions. If you are a software company, is software "hot" right now in the stock market? If so you are more likely to be able to raise money. That doesn't necessarily make sense, because early-stage investors are supposed to be betting on the *next* hot thing. Sometimes they do. But the truth is the actual mentality of fund managers is not always this forward-thinking, and the current state of the equity markets matters even in private company investing.

If you are seeking traditional bank financing, as we all know the so-called Great Recession of 2007–2009 made it nearly impossible for a number of years for average companies to obtain a regular bank loan or even receivables financing. Larger companies managing to borrow money had to pay more in interest. All the lending standards were raised and credit lines that existed for years were pulled; it was a very difficult time.

But there are periods when banks are more willing—even anxious—to lend. When the economy is strong, lending standards ease. The stock market does seem to have less of an effect on banks' views on lending, however.

If you have managed to take your company public, in addition to these you may be considering a public offering, private investment in public equity (PIPE), or similar transaction. These tend to be *highly* sensitive to stock market conditions, as you might imagine. Some investors will invest in just about any market, so long as the stock is heavily traded and they get a nice discount to the public trading price when they do. Of course, the problem is, in a down market, companies are less anxious for the ownership dilution that will come from selling stock not only when the trading price is down, but at a discount even to that.

There is no easy way to time this with the needs of your company. You require financing when you do. One thing smarter companies try to do is take advantage of good times and save as much as they can, knowing there will be another downturn at some point in the future. There are pluses and minuses to this approach. If you raise more than you need, you do further dilute your ownership and at a price that you hope is lower than the price you will raise money for in the future. If it allows you in a disciplined way to develop a reserve, in many cases the benefits of that outweigh the costs.

Industry Trends

As mentioned, being in an industry with some current Wall Street sizzle can help in improving the availability of financing. Just be careful in assuming that stock market or industry-specific "bubbles" can continue indefinitely. My simple rule: When a sector is hot and someone intelligent says, "This could last forever," that's my cue to jump. There's an old story attributed to Joseph P. Kennedy, Sr., father of the late President John F. Kennedy. According to the story, the senior Kennedy decided the market bubble of the 1920s was ending when a shoe shine boy was feeding him stock investment ideas. He sold out and made a fortune before the great stock market crash of 1929.

When have people uttered the "forever" claim in recent times? During the late 1980s and early 1990s when biotechnology stocks shot through the roof and everyone imagined an ever-growing industry based on doing well by doing good. Or consider the late 1990s when Internet stocks seemed able to rise to gargantuan levels with seemingly no end. During the mid-2000s, hundreds of Chinese companies went public in the United States with incredibly high valuations.

What happened to these bubbles? Biotech businesses lost half their value in 1992. In March 2000, the Internet stocks suddenly and unexpectedly plunged as companies burned through hundreds of millions of invested dollars with no profit to show for it and started to fail when money dried up.

In 2010 allegations of fraud and corruption in dozens of public Chinese companies wrote the future for their valuations.

Get the point? So while there is benefit to your ability to raise money if you are in an industry, geography, or sector that is then receiving a lot of Wall Street attention, do not make your plans assuming that will continue. As with the market condition as a whole, it is best to prepare for the time when "the Street" will no longer be paying attention to you.

Politics and the Regulatory Environment

I spend a good amount of time working with regulators and Congress in fashioning legislation and administrative rules that ideally work to improve smaller companies' access to capital, while maintaining an appropriate level of investor protection as well. For example, I have supported certain rule changes even though they added burdens onto dealmakers because they yielded more reliable transparency in transactions.

The problem is that the direction of the pendulum swinging for or against easing capital formation is somewhat unpredictable. In general, a Republican president and Congress are more likely to try to remove regulatory burdens on small business. But Democratic President Obama signed legislation such as the Jumpstart Our Business Startups (JOBS) Act in 2012. The JOBS Act included a number of meaningful regulatory reforms and passed Congress with unusually wide bi-partisan support. And a Republican-controlled SEC passed some very burdensome new rules relating to shell companies in 2005 and 2008 while admittedly at the same time reducing other hurdles.

In the end, the political winds drive most of the direction. There are times that a Democrat feels the need to show that he or she is helping small business and entrepreneurs. At other times, when certain problems arise like the allegations of fraud in Chinese companies, the regulators sometimes react a little too quickly to tighten things up when the pitchforks of the financial press come out, so they can show they are "doing something" about the particular problem at hand.

Another similar example is Bernard Madoff. The now-convicted and jailed multibillion dollar swindler was not intensely investigated despite six different serious complaints filed against him and his company. Why? Because he was a prominent fellow and former chairman of the Nasdaq, and, for right or wrong, many of the regulators, whether or not consciously, gave him the benefit of the doubt. It was not until a reporter was about to out the whole scheme that he told his sons what he had been doing, and the sons reported him to the authorities.

The SEC has worked very hard since the Madoff scandal to tighten up its procedures in dealing with complaints, as well as sniffing out issues before they get too out of hand. This has also meant an attitude that leans toward more regulation and oversight of broker-dealers and their related entities.

The regulatory environment can affect a company's ability to raise money in a variety of ways. When there is expectation that restrictive rules are coming, but it is unclear exactly what they might entail, some investors hold back for a short time until they find out what the new rules will entail. Of course, if your business is highly regulated, such as is true in the healthcare and biotechnology world, you have to be extra sensitive to the issues that could impede or derail your chance to raise money.

Sometimes new rules create new financing opportunities. The JOBS Act will permit companies raising money in a private offering to advertise to and solicit investors under certain circumstances. It also authorized "crowd funding," where a company can raise up to $1 million from any type of investor and any number of investors without worrying about being treated as a public offering and having to go through a time-consuming SEC review and approval of a prospectus.

Some investors become less active when we are nearing a U.S. presidential election, because the winds can shift, sometimes very dramatically, when party control in Washington shifts. Is your business tied to Wall Street or defense? You're usually better off in a Republican administration. What about healthcare or education? Probably better with the Dems. It's not clear, of course, how direct an impact it can have, and it depends on how important that regulatory environment is in your business. But it absolutely can affect how and where you raise money.

Basics of the Process

How do you actually get in contact with sources of capital, and what happens once they decide they would like to invest? That could be a whole book in itself, but we will try to summarize in the next few pages. In general, going unsolicited and unreferred to most traditional investment sources is going to be challenging.

It is best, if possible, to get to know parties who have relationships with investors or investment banking firms that are in the business of raising or investing money. Our law firm, for example, regularly introduces our entrepreneur clients to financing opportunities. We don't get paid to do it; it is simply part of the service we provide.

The challenge you can face: An average venture capital or private equity fund will review 1,000 business plans, meet with 100 of those companies, and invest in 10. Keep those odds in mind as you make the rounds. And amazingly, of the 10 they invest in, they are happy if only two or three are successful. Much like actors auditioning for a Broadway show, it is often less about your talent as it is about characteristics you don't even know they are looking for. An oft-repeated joke on the Great White Way is, "They turned me down because I didn't fit the dress."

In the investing world, a VC may say (and you wouldn't know), "We've invested in enough energy companies," "We only want companies with at least $X in revenue," or "We have to find companies that we can exit out of soon because our fund expires in three years." This can be frustrating indeed.

Making the Contact

If you are seeking government financing such as from the Small Business Administration (SBA) or an SBA-licensed investment company, here is the one place where you are most likely to receive financing even if you send in your plan over the transom without a connection. You should visit www .sba.gov, where there is a very easy-to-navigate guide to obtaining an SBA loan, or other sources of capital for that matter. The paperwork is pretty annoying but understandable, and there are eligibility requirements that you should examine, but it is all laid out on the web site.

If you are going ahead with a "friends and family" type round, again making contact is pretty easy since you already know these people. And no annoying application! Presumably you provide some kind of disclosure to them about what your plans are, though, depending on their income and net worth, this may not be legally required. Part of the question is whom to contact—ideally not just any friends and family, but those who are close enough to you and comfortable enough financially that they can afford to lose the investment they make with you without it risking your relationship with them.

I have a contact who is an investment banker. There was a social group that he was part of through a club. He believed he had an exciting investment opportunity in a retailer and invited 10 of his buddies in the group to invest. They all met the CEO, got excited, and wrote big checks, each at least $50,000 and one for $200,000. While these were financially comfortable folks, in most cases their investments were fairly significant for them.

It turns out the CEO had a criminal background relating to a securities matter that he didn't disclose, and this killed the ability for the company to raise more money or obtain bank financing, and it went under less than a year later.

The investors were not just angry at losing their money. They were angry with my investment banker contact, because a criminal background check is a common thing to do when putting together an investment opportunity, and he didn't do it. I say there *was* a social group that he *was* a part of through a club because, after this debacle, he was shamed into resigning from the club.

Any other type of financing we discuss here, including venture capital, private equity, public offering, and bank loan, requires an introduction for the greatest likelihood of success. With a bank loan, sometimes your relationship with your bank may be sufficient to get their attention, but not always. Otherwise, you need someone to get you there.

Who are those "someones"? Lawyers, accountants, consultants, and investment bankers can all be active in helping companies raise money. Finding them is a little less hard than the investors themselves. If you already have these types of contacts, great. Otherwise, friends and other business associates may have leads for people to meet.

The best way to build your database of these types of helpful connections is through networking. Find groups in your region that provide regular breakfasts or speaker series for businesspeople, hopefully focusing on earlier-stage or small businesses. Most pretty much let anyone join if they pay annual dues (most charge in the hundreds per year, but some more exclusive groups can charge thousands). Others are very picky and require a vetting process or referral before you can attend an event or become a member.

If you are not sure how to find these groups, some areas have a local business journal in which these groups run advertisements. Also ask other businesspeople in your region; they may know. In New York City, for example, *Crain's New York Business* magazine runs a regular breakfast series on small business. Of course you can also look online. There are venture groups, for example, that meet regularly on Long Island and in New Jersey—and there are many more.

You can also make good connections of this type through worthwhile charitable or even school alumni activities. Sometimes the best kind of business ties can be made with a fellow schoolmate, since there is usually a higher level of trust going in. Of course, don't get involved with a charity for business purposes; do it because you believe in and want to work for the cause. But it's not terrible if there is a side benefit of meeting worthwhile business contacts in the process.

The next thing to do is be patient. It is unlikely that you meet a plugged-in accountant at a cocktail event and she makes calls the next day on your behalf. You may know how great you are and how amazing your business opportunity is, but that doesn't mean that everyone you meet will get that right away. The number of folks that have come to my office honestly believing they have the next billion-dollar company is truly staggering. But, other than the Cougar Biotechnology example we discussed, not one of those I met in over 25 years of practice has managed that achievement.

The worst time to raise money is when you need it urgently. Do your best to plan ahead, and start making contacts now that might pay off in a year or two. But start. I always say, *you can't meet someone for the tenth time until you've met them for the first time.*

Meeting with Investors

So what happens once you finally make that contact? After several meetings, investors with strong interest issue a term sheet or a letter of intent, which outlines the deal that is planned at least at that point, the valuation they are placing on the business, and so on. A term sheet or letter of intent does not bind either party to go forward on a deal but usually binds you not to talk to other potential investors for a period of time.

Do not assume that the value they place on your business in the letter of intent is firm. It is not at all uncommon for the investor to try to lower the value after he or she completes due diligence, pointing to this issue or that of which he or she was not aware. And yes, it is very rare for this to go the other way and good things lead to an increase in the value (shocking, I know).

Then usually comes a "due diligence" review of your business by the potential investor. This may entail your setting up an online data room with all the key documents that the company is a party to, important contracts, intellectual property, and so forth. Most investors will spend quite a bit of time meeting with you, understanding your challenges, and gauging your determination and personality.

They may want to talk to your customers, suppliers, lower-level managers, and maybe even competitors. (They usually do this in a manner that does not reveal their interest in your company.) This process may take anywhere from 30 to 90 days, depending on the investor. A small handful of investors are willing to sign a binding investment agreement before this begins, but with the completion of the investment being subject to due diligence being completed satisfactorily, most will not.

The documentation process once a "go" decision has been reached after due diligence also varies. The Small Business Administration (SBA) has a formal application process, and if you are lucky enough to be approved, you receive a standard set of documents. You still should have an attorney review things, however, if for no other reason than to make sure you understand what part of your life (and often your spouse's as well) you are signing away.

This is similar with bank loans. The joke among bank lawyers is "We sent the company the documents and told them they can make any two changes they want other than the business terms." The documents are pretty much not changeable, but again, a lawyer should walk you through the provisions that burden you. One key is the "events of default" section, which lets them accelerate the repayment of the loan. Most bank documents include something like "We are feeling uncomfortable about you" as an event of default, which is the same as saying, if they want to call the loan, they will.

Also with bank loans, check if there is a penalty for early repayment of the loan. Often there is, because the bank is in the business of charging you interest and does not want that to end until the loan matures. This might be something you can try to negotiate if it is important to have that flexibility, but most banks will not.

When you are involved in an offering to friends and family, as indicated, you may or may not choose to prepare a disclosure document for them. In this or any other type of offering, the more information you give people, the less they will have to complain about later.

It all comes down to how big an insurance policy you want to buy (figuratively) against future claims if things don't go well. Most of those claims say, "You didn't tell me X. If you had told me X, I would not have invested." That doesn't mean they win a claim against you saying that. In most cases they have to prove that you intentionally withheld information. So you can choose to prepare what is typically called a Private Placement Memorandum (PPM). Sometimes it is called an Information Memorandum.

The PPM usually includes an eight- to 10-page description of the business, marketing, competition, and the like. Then it lays out a similarly long list of risk factors that an investor should consider when subscribing. If written well, an unsophisticated investor would read the risk factors and run from the deal. In addition, customarily management biographies, a summary of executive compensation, and use of the proceeds from the offering are included.

If all of the investors' income or net worth is sufficient, however, subject to the "insurance policy" argument previously noted, you can simply hand them a standard subscription document without a PPM. That agreement should contain key statements, or representations, from the investor such as that they have had any questions answered, had access to any information they needed, have a certain level of sophistication, and understand there is great risk and they can lose all their money. Again, use a good lawyer when putting this together.

Things get a bit more complex in dealing with angels, venture capitalists, private equity, and PIPE investors. They more commonly require pretty comprehensive "purchase agreements" that have you making 35–40 representations to them about your business. These can include attaching a bunch of schedules laying out things like compensation plans, capitalization, related entities, and insurance policies. Then they typically require your attorney to issue a legal opinion that pretty much everything important is kosher. (Banks usually require this, too.)

These investors also may have additional separate agreements governing things like registration rights, (their right to have their shares included in any public offering so that they can be immediately tradable), and their right to board seats. You can easily be dealing with 100 pages of documents to get through.

If the investor is receiving some kind of preferred stock or a convertible note of some kind, then additional documents are needed for that, either a state filing outlining the terms of the preferred stock or the actual form of convertible note.

Now, let's outline the different types of financing.

The Six Methods

There are six main sources of financing for a growing business. In the brief discussion of these in the last chapter we focused on the right fit with your company, in particular which method yields the investor more control and more ownership. Here, in no particular order, we talk more about the commonly discussed advantages and disadvantages of each method.

Bootstrap

"Bootstrap" is a term coming from the old days when most people wore boots and there were loops around the side, usually made of leather, to help get the boots on. People were well regarded for "pulling themselves up by their own bootstraps." The term "booting" a computer also is derived from this.

A common way to help a business grow is by allowing the profits it generates to fund expansion or new opportunities, or bootstrapping. What does this really involve? First, you need to determine what needs you may have to finance new investments, marketing, or the like. Then you need to hope that the business will indeed provide sufficient resources to get through the list.

Alternatively, when you raise outside money, you can define a need and then, hopefully, raise the right amount of money in a predictable way to accomplish the stated goals. Of course there is the tremendous amount of time you have to spend going out to raise money, and it ultimately may be unavailable or on unacceptable terms after all that effort.

This is one of the reasons some entrepreneurs choose to fund things themselves. Another form of bootstrapping is when the owner puts his or her own money into the business. This is not the same as using the profits as you go, although in effect business profits you reinvest in the company are your money because you would have otherwise been able to pull the money out.

But there is something more dramatic about emptying your bank account (or, for others, running up the credit cards or home equity line of credit) to enhance the risk you have in building your business. For some, psychologically, taking a smaller profit home is not the same as writing the check from savings.

The advantages to this approach include maximizing your freedom and control. There's no bank telling you to strengthen your balance sheet, no venture capitalist with veto power over things, and no pressure from Wall Street to perform. For some, this is the main reason they started a business—to be answerable to no one.

By bootstrapping you also retain full ownership in the business. When one of my clients sold his $25 million revenue business for $18 million, most of it went in his pocket (well, until the IRS took its share). All too often companies are sold with the bulk of the proceeds going to the investors and a relatively small percentage making its way back to the people who toiled to build the company.

Bootstrapping also allows you to decide the timing of the exit scenario, if at all. Some entrepreneurs have no interest in "monetizing" ownership in the company. Investors pretty much all are seeking the way out at some point. If you would rather think of your company as your life's work, and not a four- to six-year push leading to a sale, then having outside investors may not work for you.

This can be particularly true in a family business, where there is a desire for ownership and control to be passed to future generations. Here it is not easy to convince an investor that an exit is likely. Family businesses are particularly known for bootstrapping; often the big talk at the Thanksgiving table is why Grandpa took 50 percent of the company's profits last year to open new stores that may not be successful, but then the next year all are praising Grandpa for his vision (hopefully!).

There is, of course, a downside of bootstrapping. When you take profits out of the business rather than seek outside investors, there are fewer profits to put in your pocket. If you can afford to earn less money while the business is building that's great, but this is simply not possible for all entrepreneurs. Betting it all may be fine, but for how long?

The other challenge with bootstrapping is its uncertainty. As mentioned, you simply cannot predict each year or quarter what profits may be available to fund the company's growth. If you have deep pockets personally or family money that is pretty much available when needed, this may not be an issue for you. For most, this uncertainty can make this approach more difficult.

And of course, no matter how much money you pull out of the business for the future, it may never be enough compared to outside money that could be raised. Companies that could raise $10 million at a time from investors but are very unlikely ever to generate that kind of profit to fund things internally could find their growth hampered by the limitation on available funds.

In the end, weigh the freedom and control versus maximizing certainty and growth potential to see what works in your situation.

Government Financing

The U.S., state, city, and local governments all have programs that provide loans, investments, or in some cases direct grants to small businesses. Each has different standards for you to qualify for help or not. Most states have programs that favor women- or minority-owned businesses. They are generally good at spotting "fake" attempts to stick a nominal female or minority person in an ownership position, so it's not a good idea to try that.

The U.S. Small Business Administration, as well as investment companies authorized by the SBA, make loans to small businesses, usually no more than $1 million, and most significantly less. As mentioned previously, there is a lengthy application process, but a number of lucky companies do receive financing.

Often smaller states can be more proactive in looking to help and protect local businesses. A client of mine in the healthcare space in a small southern state has tapped loans with very favorable terms from several state government agencies. These state lenders spend time meeting with the company, studying their financial statements, and making sure they are financially sound. It is good for the state in encouraging job growth and keeping companies from moving elsewhere.

Unlike with the SBA and larger states, political connections seem to be beneficial in getting the attention of the local lending agencies, though of course this varies by jurisdiction. This then puts companies in the business of taking time to curry political favor locally. Some are willing to put this time (and sometimes money) in, not others.

A loan from a government agency has certain benefits. Much like with a bank, the loan does not take any business ownership away. So if you believe that your growth will continue, especially with the new financing, and you will be able to service the debt, you may determine it is better to do that than to dilute your ownership in your company. Some government lenders do take small equity stakes in the form of warrants to buy your stock later, but in general these are barely noticeable in the dilution to existing shareholders.

Government lenders also tend to be a bit more flexible than a typical bank lender when trouble arises. If it looks like you will not make a payment, or you somehow go into default on the loan, chances are greater with a government lender that the lender will try to work with you. Government lenders are more likely to try to address the situation without declaring a default and coming after whatever assets they have chosen to attach a lien to in order to protect their interests. Since their primary goal is to assist small business, rather than make money on the loan, it is in their interest to try to make things work a bit more than your average bank.

On the flip side, many government (and most SBA) loans require personal guaranties from company principals and, in many cases, their spouses. Some banks may require guaranties, but they rarely if ever tie up spouses who are uninvolved in the business. With a personal guaranty, of course, an individual promises to pay back the loan if the company cannot. One of the primary purposes of forming a business entity is to shield the business owners from personal responsibility for the debts and obligations of the business. Once you decide to guarantee an obligation, some of that benefit goes away.

But in many cases the guaranty is simply unavoidable. The spousal guaranty, however, further complicates things. I had a client whose husband had built a business and borrowed $1 million from the SBA. The lender required the husband and my client, his wife, to sign personally. They also gave the SBA a mortgage on their house to protect the loan.

Unfortunately, things in both the business and marriage did not fare well. The company went out of business, and the husband sought a divorce, moved to Puerto Rico, and declared personal bankruptcy, under laws then essentially relieving him of his personal guaranty. The only thing left was the lien on the house that the wife was living in, on top of her personal promise to pay. My client struggled for the next seven years to restructure, then pay off the loan. Yes, she did have to sell her house. If she didn't work things out, her credit would have been destroyed—all because of a business she had no part in run by a husband who left her.

Bank Financing

Like government loans, bank loans have the benefit of not diluting your ownership—that is, if you are lucky enough to qualify and if banks are indeed lending. Much of this depends on the economic cycle. When times and the economy are strong, banks tend to be more open to lending. Of course, in a recession they tend to tighten up their lending standards. Then in times of crisis, such as in 2009–2010, they all but shut down lending except for their largest and most loyal customers, or those who provide dramatically strong collateral to back up a loan.

Even after you are lucky enough to get that loan or credit line, during the most difficult times, they may decide simply not to renew longstanding lines of credit or loans that expire. I had a client that was a metals distributor with a 10-year relationship with a major money center bank. The company had a $500,000 line of credit that was essential for cash flow when ordering supplies and waiting for customers to pay. The company's financial performance had been strong and unchanged for five years when the bank unceremoniously informed my client that he had 60 days to pay the loan and that it was not going to be renewed.

My client was lucky on two levels. First, he had sufficient personal assets to contribute to the business to pay the loan. Second, he was able to restructure certain elements of the business to manage for about a year by stretching out payables, being tougher on customer payment cycles, and, frankly, cutting some costs in their warehouse.

My guess is he didn't feel very lucky, however. But if this was not possible, this self-protective act by the bank could literally have meant the end of his business. After that year the economy was a little stronger and he negotiated a new line with a different bank.

So if you do go forward with a bank loan, do your best to be ready to repay, rather than refinance it, when it comes due. Also, don't assume another bank will just come along and replace them. That said, there are some benefits to a bank loan. They don't always require personal guaranties if you can provide strong collateral such as inventory and receivables, and as noted, they rarely require spousal guaranties or mortgages on your home.

Again, there is the benefit of no dilution of company ownership. The debt does sit on your balance sheet as an obligation, which does not always please others who may partner with your company on things, as well as potential equity investors. The repayment of the debt also burdens your cash flow, as interest and principal payments are taken out of your profits.

Some banks band together to deal with many states' requirement that banks put money back into their local community. These so-called "community reinvestment" obligations lead to microloans and some small grants that banks will make to smaller companies. I used to represent a consortium of New York banks that joined to establish a fund to help satisfy their respective obligations to so reinvest.

The community reinvestment fund was run by a savvy Wall Street veteran. He recognized that the main purpose of the fund was to help the community, but he had a real sense that the banks were very hopeful that they might actually make some money here. He loaned $500,000 to $1 million at a time to young companies, getting not only money back with interest but also an equity ownership in the form of warrants, giving them the right to buy a small percentage of the company at a specified price in the future. The fund did *not* require any personal guaranties.

The fund was an interesting combination of a traditional bank loan and something closer to the government lender's attitude of just trying to help small business. The head of the fund was patient when companies defaulted, worked to restructure troubled loans, and spent time trying to help companies get on their feet when difficulties arose. But his patience was clearly lower than a government lender.

If a bank community reinvestment lending opportunity arises with legitimate folks, that might be worth taking a look at, as sort of a middle ground between bank and government lending.

Friends and Family

A popular method of financing an early-stage company is simply to pass the hat around to people whom know you personally, as well as your family members. We talked earlier about some of the perils of being in business with family. As with friends, just make sure that, if nothing else, you ensure that money they invest is truly money they can lose with no effect on their lifestyle, retirement, or attitude toward you.

This method of financing has decided advantages. First, as most of the investors are not likely to be professional investors, you can generally have a simpler and, frankly, more company-favorable structure to the investment. Most may be doing it for fun, or out of friendship, and not as much hoping for a big score. So as we discussed in the last chapter they are not as worried about that extra 2–3 percent ownership that a more seasoned investor may seek.

Another advantage of a friends and family (F&F) fundraise is that, in our litigious society, these folks are simply less likely to come after you or your company if the investment is unsuccessful. We often talk with law clients not as much about whether the company would have the risk of being sued successfully and actually being liable for doing something, but rather the simple risk of being sued.

This "litigation risk" is annoying and unpredictable, and does not result from events within the company's control. As some patients sue doctors for medical malpractice when a treatment is unsuccessful, even where there is no evidence the doctor did anything other than use appropriate protocol, some investors simply sue when they lose money and worry about the proof later.

Why do they do this? In some cases it's simply out of anger at the failure of the investment. In other cases it is more calculated and designed to force the company into some sort of settlement, even in the absence of wrong-doing, so the company can avoid hefty legal fees even defending a case it knows it can win. The friends and family round of financing comes with a safer feeling with respect to litigation risk.

There are, of course, disadvantages to this approach. First, you can typically only go to the F&F well once. Multiple rounds of financing from people close to you is not likely or realistic in most cases. Second, as indicated previously, they are not likely to be business-savvy folks who can actually help your business, as some professional investors can be.

Last, despite all your efforts to make sure that these people who are close to you and invest in your company understand they may lose everything, they still might get angry if things don't go well. So no matter what people say going in, when they lose money, some people simply have an emotionally negative response even where it is money they can afford to lose.

Angel, Venture Capital, and Private Equity

Here you are looking at professional investors in the startup, early, and late stages, respectively. Angel investors are typically individuals either with a good amount of investing experience or a strong managerial background. They tend to invest personal cash or family money. Some are organized into groups; others prefer to work on their own. In most major regions there are regular gatherings of these groups, and you can try to become a company that has the luck to present at one of their meetings. (Some of them charge a fee to do so.)

The typical venture capital firm, whose money tends to come in after the angel round, is run by super-smart Ivy League MBAs who are very savvy in the world of finance. As smart as they are, they often have a "herd" mentality when it comes to investing trends. When the Internet surged as a venture investment, most got in because others did, not necessarily because they had carefully analyzed the economics of the individual opportunities or the sector. Unfortunately it took years for many of them to recover from the losses that hit them when the Internet boom went to bust in early 2000.

Venture funds are formed by raising money typically from large institutions, pension funds, and very wealthy individuals. It is common for funds to exceed $100 million in capital. This is good for the managers because they typically receive a fee equal to 2 percent of that capital to run their business, unrelated to the success of their investments. This allows them to pay bills, and a basic salary for themselves and what is usually a very small team of analysts. They also usually get 20 percent of the profits earned from investing the money entrusted to them. That, of course, is where they hope the big money will come from.

Private equity investors tend to straddle between making minority investments in later-stage companies and doing actual buyouts of more mature companies, including buying public companies and taking them private. In fact, what some used to call leveraged buyout funds have been pretty much re-branded as private equity firms. Often the venture funds hand off deals to these later-stage investors when they get past a point that the "VC" can continue to fund.

In general private equity investors take lower risks than VC or angel types, but as a result they generally expect potential returns that are not as outsized as those for the earlier-stage investors. Buying a mature, profitable, growing company is not the same as investing in a pre-revenue company with an exciting patent and strong management team.

There are a number of similarities in dealing with these professional investors. As pointed out previously, they really become your partners. They can bring great ideas. A number of these firms have added partners with real operating experience to strengthen that ability to add value to the business of their portfolio companies.

However, they do typically require seats on your board, and can give you agita if they are displeased with the direction of the company; generally, as mentioned, they hold veto powers over major decisions. Also don't expect a quick check. As mentioned, once they are seriously interested it is not unusual to have a three- to four-month due diligence and documentation process before you sign and actually get the dough.

These investors almost always take equity, although some do take debt that can convert into equity. This happens more in down markets, frankly, since it's better for the investor to have the best of both worlds of protecting their downside by getting their debt repaid if things go badly but being able to fully convert into stock ownership as the company grows and succeeds.

Assuming any debt gets converted, there is no debt to repay, which is good. In addition, these types of investors will be much more likely to be able to fund future rounds of financing, which is not typically available in friends and family or even most bank loan situations. If you are okay with some of the restrictions these types of investors place, there can be a number of benefits as well.

Initial Public Offering (IPO) or Public Company (PIPE) Financing

Many companies do indeed go public in large part to raise money. In fact, it is easily the number-one reason companies seek a public listing for their stock. As discussed in great detail in my books on reverse mergers, since 1999 it has been nearly impossible for a smaller company to complete a traditional IPO as a way to raise money. Some lucky few have gotten through, but the statistics are pretty stark.

As mentioned earlier, in 2012 the Congress passed and President Obama signed into law the Jumpstart Our Business Startups (JOBS) Act. With such a wonderful acronym, no one dared vote against it! The hope, among other things, was to implement certain changes to make initial public offerings more attractive and a bit less burdensome. Unfortunately since then through this writing, there has not yet been a rush of new IPOs into the marketplace.

Since the IPO market effectively shut down, thousands of companies, still looking to be public, have opted for reverse mergers. As described earlier, in a reverse merger a company goes public by combining with a public shell company. With a shady past, reverse mergers are now legitimate and popular if you work with the right people, even though some alleged trouble with Chinese companies going public in the United States led to some bad press and SEC tightening of regulation in the early 2010s.

If you are merging with a shell, there is still a way to raise money while going public, with a so-called PIPE investment. It provides fast cash and involves an investment by a hedge fund or an institutional investor at a discount to your stock's public trading price. PIPEs go in and out of popularity depending on the appetite for investors to seek liquidity or not in their public investing. If an immediate ability to sell is important, a PIPE is not ideal since it normally takes about four to six months before an investor can sell into the public market.

Other methods of investment into public companies, including shelf offerings, allow a public company to give an investor immediately tradable shares at a discount to the public trading price as a way to raise money for the company. These are very popular, but unfortunately currently may only be used by companies with a market value in excess of $75 million, or any company trading on the "national" exchanges such as Nasdaq, NYSE AMEX, and NYSE Euronext. So for the companies below that market value and not on a major exchange, the PIPE is the best option.

Despite the challenges of PIPEs, they are an efficient method of financing, especially for a company that seeks to go public but does not qualify for, or want to take the various risks involving, a traditional IPO. Many companies choose this method of going public because PIPE investors impose few restrictions on a company's activities and are almost always sold at a stock price that would be higher than a price that an investor would pay if the company remained private.

However, while PIPEs are popular with companies, the stock market isn't always thrilled, and in many cases a company's stock price declines after a PIPE investment is made. This is because investors don't always like the often-deep discount to the market price that is offered to the investor, diluting the ownership of everyone else. But for most companies that are this small and public, the need to raise money pretty much always trumps maintaining stock price in the short run.

If you consider going public, think carefully. Being public is expensive, increases your risk of lawsuits, exposes both the good and bad aspects of your company's business (including your compensation and your financial results), and forces you to feel pressure to perform for Wall Street each quarter, sometimes to the detriment of your long-term plans.

But there are many advantages, such as easier access to capital, greater ability to complete acquisitions for growth, more PR for your company's activities, an ability to reward executives with valuable stock options, and a path to liquidity of ownership for every investor, including you as entrepreneur and owner. I always tell clients: If you can benefit from being publicly held, and can bear the costs of doing so, it is worth serious consideration.

Therefore . . .

Here we learned that the economy, the stock market, your industry, and the regulatory environment all play a role in the relative availability of and terms under which you can get financing for your growing business. We covered making contact with financing sources and laid out a bit of the process for getting the deal done.

As to the six key methods of financing, try to assess in an ideal world what type of investment makes the most sense for your company, its growth plans, your personality and culture, and your confidence in achieving your business plan. All these play a role in determining the most likely successful path to bringing in capital.

Of course if you need the money and there is one type of investor standing there and no others, your choice becomes much simpler. Just make sure, if you are down to that one choice, that you know it is worth continuing with the business against whatever challenges may arise with that source of financing.

It is not easy for an entrepreneur to pull off the success of my client mentioned at the beginning of the chapter in growing a business by your bootstraps. If you can really pull it off, of course, it is the path of least resistance. But even then, be sure that going it alone is your best path. If not, take a hard look at what fresh outside capital can bring to your venture.

CHAPTER 8

Too Pooped to Produce?

Common Causes of Exhaustion and How to Recover

The next two chapters, much like Chapter 4 on work/less work balance, focus on both the psychological and physical burdens that building an entrepreneurial business can place on you. This chapter is about the exhaustion that can creep in; the next one is more about what happens when the business grows to a point that it is less entrepreneurial and, for some, boredom sets in. We will examine strategies hopefully to prevent or at least successfully deal with these pressures.

As we have discussed, most entrepreneurs don't know much about punching time clocks. They work nights and weekends because they are focused, determined, and excited about the business. They feel tremendous pressure to show their family, friends, coworkers, business contacts, and the whole world how successful they can be.

Even if work/less work balance is achieved somewhat, and certainly in cases where it does not, at some point it can all take its toll, even if—and in some cases because—the business is successful. Burnout is an occupational hazard for all driven entrepreneurs.

We often compare being at the helm of a growing business to being a marathon runner. Many runners do not define success by how fast they complete a 26-mile race or even if they complete it. Some say it is as much about the journey of the race itself that makes the experience worthwhile. For so many entrepreneurs, a major challenge is remembering to enjoy the ride. Too many forget to savor the moments along the way to success. As there are for the marathon runner, there are both physical and mental challenges.

Yes, you train for the long race for four to six months. But when you are beyond mile 20 and your entire body wants to shut down, what keeps you going? It's up to your mental determination.

Part of that is making sure to savor even the small successes along the way. Making a great hire. Scoring a big customer. Signing that first office or store lease. Landing a strong round of capital. Getting in the door of a major new contact. Writing yourself a nice cash distribution check. Even when that business card arrives that says "President" on it.

But don't celebrate too much! As mentioned earlier, I remember at the tender age of 23 buying a radio station. My partner and I first faced the challenge of finding the right station after rejecting several. Then we had to negotiate the right deal to purchase after being unsuccessful at doing so with others. Next, we two kids worked to raise the money from investors to complete the purchase and operate. Finally, we had to negotiate the legal documentation with lawyers who ultimately charged us triple what we had thought. That was quite an achievement in itself!

We were so excited at least to be operating the station until we looked at each other and realized, "Oh, now we have to make money somehow." It was quite the sobering moment. While we did operate for four years, we eventually had to sell the station at a loss. We learned many lessons that I used in my later, more successful ventures, but a loss it was. So enjoy everything along the way but at all times with your eyes ahead on the challenges yet to come.

How do you keep going when things get rough? You can tell I have a young child when I take an example from *Finding Nemo*. In the movie, comedienne Ellen DeGeneres portrays Dory, a forgetful blue tang fish. Dory's mantra when things are challenging is simple: "Just keep swimming." For that marathon runner, maybe it's "Just keep running." For the exhausted entrepreneur: "Just keep plugging." Or, as a friend once said to me, "Just get up the next day and do it again."

Life brings us challenges, and we should do all we can to appreciate the path of life dealing with those challenges. When burnout wins despite every effort, go back to the drawing board. Think about the causes, the preventative strategies that will keep it from happening again, and how to get back on track when you do get exhausted. We'll start with some of the causes.

Causes of Burnout

Dictionary.com includes one of its definitions of "burnout" as a noun meaning "someone no longer effective on the job." Of course in my growing-up days in the 1970s, teens had a little different meaning for the word (in fact "Burnout" was the official nickname of one of my classmates), but the concept is the same. There can be many different causes of business burnout; here are a few.

Spousal/Family Pressure

Spousal pressure on an entrepreneur can be significantly daunting for some. Not everyone is excited about the huge risk their spouse takes in giving up steady income for tremendous uncertainty. Yet many don't want to stand in the way of their spouse's dream, even if they have significant doubts. So they suppress any expression of concern and initially support their spouse's foray into entrepreneurship.

This pressure is enhanced even more if the non-entrepreneur spouse does not work, or the couple has children and the financial needs of the family grow. Some, even unconsciously, may criticize or give backhanded compliments. When you land a big customer and your spouse says, "Good, because we need it," you may have an issue.

When you take a rare, needed afternoon off, do you hear, "I don't see how you have the ability to take time off when we are still only making [X] percent of what you made when you had a salary"? In some ways this can be even worse if you have some great years and then things contract. That's when the non-supportive spouse may start hinting around at you going back to the W-2 life of an employee, even if you're still doing pretty well.

Do you find yourself avoiding the discussion with your spouse if things are turning down and your take-home has taken a hit? The toll this enhanced pressure takes on your energy level and ability to function can be significant. Presumably it's a motivator—this desire to please the doubting spouse—but it more often ends up sapping rather than providing energy.

Spouses working together face different issues causing stress and burnout. Which spouse is working harder? Which one is bringing more to the business? Which one is more controlling of the two? How do you handle time off? Who takes care of the kids? Does a downturn in business get you to work together harder or spend time blaming each other? Does constant togetherness bring you closer or leave you always arguing?

Others find that family issues get in the way. A friend of mine has a disabled son, and he and his wife dutifully deal with his constant care while also raising two other children. He ultimately gave up on his attempt to start his own service business when he realized it just was not possible for him to devote the time necessary to build the business while also attending to his son, who was obviously the greater priority. So he went back to a comfortable, albeit less fulfilling, job that gave him a bit more time flexibility and less added stress to what he was already dealing with.

A good friend of mine started his own accounting firm after about 10 years of working with the largest U.S. firms. He knew he was ready to start on his own and had a good initial group of clients. His wife, a full time homemaker with two young kids, told him she was fully behind his effort, though privately had significant doubts. She later told him that if she really believed he would start his own firm she would have said no. Given this attitude, all through his efforts to build a practice, while she truly tried to be supportive, she was never satisfied with any of his success.

If he made more than the previous year, she would ask what it would take to make even more the next year. If his income dropped, she would say things like "We can't live on that." His response, of course, was, "We have to live on that." These were not easy discussions. If they did take vacation because she felt the kids needed it, she expected him to be up in the hotel room at least three or four hours a day working. It finally got to a breaking point. Unfortunately, both his firm and his marriage ended. He returned to a mid-sized accounting firm, at least bringing business with him and enjoying the perks of a partner, and asked his wife for a divorce, in good part because of her abject failure to support him in his attempt to build his own firm.

As has been discussed throughout this book, family pressures can be particularly burdensome on a female entrepreneur. As we touched on in Chapter 4, most women see themselves as primary caretakers of their children even if both spouses work full-time. In some cases a female entrepreneur, especially if working from home, has some ability to control her schedule and try to work around her kids' obligations.

While one would think this is easy to do, it is not. Customers want to speak when it's best for them. Your supplier in London has to hear from you by 5 PM their time. That proposal for new business has to get done this weekend. In addition, working at home is not necessarily a panacea; in fact it can enhance the stress. There is a constant reminder 50 feet away that you are choosing to work instead of taking time with the kids. This can be exacerbated if you reach a point where you need to be more involved in caring for an elderly parent or relative as well.

This can lead to resentment and frustration with her husband if he feels she is not pulling her weight, or, worse, he secretly wishes she would just give up the new business because it takes her away too much.

The wife of a friend of mine, himself very successful, started a unique business that required a tremendous effort at promotion. Because of the business she was often hobnobbing with celebrities, traveling quite a bit, and seemingly enjoying a bit of the party lifestyle as well—or at least that's how my friend felt. He began to be resentful, even worried that she might be straying from him. He asked her to travel less and spend more time with him and their two children, but she told him he was being unfair and refused. Eighteen months later they were divorced. She continued with her business.

The ideal entrepreneur spouse is 100 percent supportive 100 percent of the time. This is a person to whom you can turn in sharing exciting moments as well as the difficulties, and a person who does not judge your performance but is simply there for you either with helpful suggestions, maybe even a little back rub, and, most importantly, an attitude that projects "How do we deal with this together?"

The reality is it is nearly impossible for anyone to be 100 percent of anything 100 percent of the time. So as you head out on your own, accept that even the most amazing and supportive spouse may have his or her own moments of frustration and doubt. And realize that your spouse's reactions to your business can indeed lead to increased stress and likelihood of burnout.

Unexpected Business Pressures or Stagnation

Those of you with kids, answer this: Before you had children, did you look at other people with kids and think, "I can do that"? While having and raising children is possibly life's greatest achievement (my mother would say it is only surpassed when your children have kids), it is an overwhelming and all-consuming adventure for which life gives you little preparation.

Most first-time entrepreneurs will tell you it is the same with starting your own business. You have good experience in your industry. You look at the bosses at your job making the tough decisions and know you could do better if given the chance. You know you have the determination and drive. And yet when you finally get your own business, it is more challenging than you ever could have expected.

I felt this way when I started my first law firm after seven years slogging it in the large firms. I had spent as much time as I could building a network and bringing in a few clients. At first I was so excited to have exclusive control of my schedule and be able to focus on building the business.

The good news: In the first year we far exceeded our expectations. We planned on losing money in year one but managed to each earn a small salary instead. The bad news: Getting there was much harder than either my partner or I ever expected. Before we knew it, we'd both started sprouting gray hair even though we were in our early 30s!

We had to learn so much in such a short time. We had to learn about the basic mechanics of setting up a business, including how to manage our payroll and file taxes. We had to find an office, get furniture, set up phones and computers, and so on; it was all new. We were reasonably intelligent attorneys and found this more than a little challenging!

This was nothing compared to going out and getting new business in the door. It wasn't for lack of trying. We busted our rear ends contacting everyone and pushing every way we could. We were thrilled with the business that came but equally, or maybe even more, annoyed and frustrated by what did not. There was often no rhyme or reason, and at times we lost business that we tried the hardest for and landed clients for whom we made virtually no effort.

I encourage new attorneys in our firm now to try to do the same—build a network, and bring in clients. I do it for many reasons that are good for them and our firm. One main reason is so they see how hard it is to pull off. My profession is full of many attorneys who attempted to build their own practice but failed. I'm proud to say that I was one of the lucky ones who broke out of the pack and did well. But it was really, really hard.

So you start with this added and unexpected pressure almost automatically. Throughout the entrepreneurial experience, lots more unexpected things can happen. You lose a key customer or employee. You face a damaging lawsuit. Your 10-month effort to land a big client comes up empty. Your bank calls your credit line or loan. A government agency starts questioning something you have done. The IRS or state taxing authority gets on your back.

Sometimes the exhaustion comes when the business simply cannot break out of a zone of activity. You do $X per year in revenue and it just does not seem to want to go up from there. For some this may be fine. I had a client who supplied industrial equipment doing $110 million a year in sales and about $8 million in profit. The business continued at this level for about 10 years. No one complained since a relatively small number of people shared that $8 million each year.

For most entrepreneurs, stagnation, even if greatly profitable, is death. Some say if you don't move forward you are moving backward. The enormous self-imposed pressure a business owner can place on him- or herself when the business stalls can really burden an individual (constant second guessing and self-analysis, loss of sleep, you name it).

Then there are situations in an entrepreneurial environment where the entire business seems to be heading downward. If you see a steady decline in revenue and profits over a period of more than a year or two, of course that presents a serious problem. This certainly enhances stress and frustration across the board.

I wasn't present to run the radio station I bought, but my partner, who was, got truly burned out by the time we finally sold. He later went back to law school, and is now a senior U.S. government official and, for him, happily past his entrepreneurial experience.

So yes, when the unexpected happens, so does more exhaustion. Business is hard!

Surprising Success

There was a great commercial in the 1990s about a new Internet company. They had spent a few years getting ready to launch a site to sell products. The commercial comes at the moment the site is being turned on. After a short initial span of inaction, first one, then 10 orders come. Then 30, 100, 1,000, and the numbers just go through the roof from there. Suddenly the initially excited executives give each other blank stares, as if to say, "How are we going to handle this?"

This is the classic "good problem": having so much business you can't even manage it. However, as I always tell my staff, a good problem is still a problem. The streets are littered with businesses that did not survive for failure to deliver on promises to more customers than they were equipped to service.

Some of the busiest, most overwhelmed entrepreneurs I know are those who face the greatest amount of success. You would think they are the most organized and with the deepest team to get things done. This just isn't always the case. It is said that man plans and God laughs. Whether it's underperformance or tremendous success, in both cases it is likely that the growth of the business did not go as planned. This can cause stress even when things are going great.

In a service business like mine, satisfying clients has a number of key components. Of course, the quality of the work and the positive attitude of those doing it are very important. Clients also want a fair price for the work being done. They also want the fastest possible turnaround of the work so that their project can move forward. The amount of business I have taken from capable competitors simply because they were either too busy or too disorganized to service the client in a timely manner is a little scary.

When a law firm, accounting firm, or similar business gets unexpectedly successful, a conundrum develops. How does it start? I begin to get calls from clients that their project is not progressing at the pace they expected. The seemingly simple response is to hire more people to handle the extra work.

Yet that simple response is the furthest from simple, as the analysis must go further. Yes, we are extra busy now, but will that be the case six months from now after we hire more people? Yes, we could just fire people at that point, but no one wants to plan that way. So in general most businesses like mine allow a period of time with extra work to develop before committing to add more people. Does this create stress? You think?

And even when a decision is made to hire, the process of advertising, interviewing, finding, and then training the new person is very time-consuming. There is real uncertainty, regardless of the promise after the interview process, as to whether your new employee will perform and fit in. Remember our discussion about how every hire in a smaller, growing company is critical and worth the extra time to do so. While this is good advice, it can be part of what leads to simple extreme fatigue.

You may be an Internet-based company, highly scalable. But when zillions more folks sign on, will you face downtime? Slower responses? Even, heaven forbid, crashes? Do you need to invest in more servers? More cloud capacity? (Sorry, my tech-speak is limited.)

For other companies involved in technology or manufacturing, the issues are similar. If we have tons and tons of orders and our manufacturer can handle them barely, but their delivery times are going to be delayed, do you live with that? Do you add another manufacturer? Maybe try to develop your own production capability? These are vexing questions.

Even surprising success can lead to developing a weariness with the business.

Burnout Prevention

There are a number of things you can do before signs of exhaustion creep in or overtake you. Some overlap with our earlier discussion of work/less work balance, but will be repeated here as well. (Some of you ADD-type entrepreneurs need to hear these more than once!) Each of the items covered here also can be used to deal with burnout when it shows up as well, but better to turn to them early, much like taking vitamins and getting regular checkups to prevent disease.

Adjust the Plan—Up or Down

This would seem obvious, but to many it just doesn't come to them. You had a plan—a vision for the success of the business when you started or even a number of years in. Many feel strangely tied to that plan. In hindsight you usually come to realize that every plan has flaws, and if this is your first startup, maybe even many flaws.

As noted, exhaustion can come from trying to run a business with Plan A when business in fact is doing half of what Plan A provided or, just as difficult, when it is doing twice what Plan A expected. One way of coping with stress is to tackle head on the source of the stress. Simple: redo the plan.

You still don't know for sure what the future will bring. Most entrepreneurs privately laugh when you ask what revenues they expect in the coming year or, if they have a budget, whether they expect to achieve it. Most, frankly, really have no clue. It is not their fault, but smaller businesses inherently involve more uncertainties and sometimes dramatic ups and downs in performance.

But inside that business the entrepreneur must trudge on and operate. If you see business taking what even appears to be a fairly steady uptick, start asking what additional resources are necessary to handle that, make sure you have the funds to invest in those resources, and then do it.

If things are not going great, and there is no immediate upturn in the cards as best as you can see, think about what cutbacks in overhead might be achievable. For most, avoiding employee layoffs is a great priority; for others, the payroll is the first to get hit. Just keep morale in mind when making these decisions. You worked hard to get the right people in the door; make sure the ones who are left are still happy even though you got rid of others.

This can be a good time to talk with helpful advisors—your counsel, accountant, consultant if you have one. And yes, a supportive spouse often can provide useful guidance. If the plan is to be adjusted, make sure you have run the thoughts by your key employees to make sure they feel they have had some input into the decision, and because they may well have some good ideas since they also have been experiencing some of the same frustration that you have been.

When your plan is adjusted to accommodate a different reality, there is a decent chance your stress level will be somewhat alleviated. Yes, you can now handle that extra business. You can now manage with less business and still make a living.

Take a Break

When I say "take a break," I do not mean the regular breaks and vacations that every worker should be taking. This is the "I'm worried that my stress could lead to burnout and need a major mental break from the business or I'm simply not going to make it" moment. Too often an entrepreneur will tell his or her spouse, "Maybe next year, when the business is doing better" or "Maybe next year, when I'm not managing so much unexpected business."

What type of break is most likely to reduce your stress level can be different for different people. For some, a few days relaxing at a beach somewhere can do wonders. Others with the adventure gene would love a little time hiking or whitewater rafting. I know others who are into seeing the world and sightseeing. And yes, for some even a trip to Disney World with the kids can help keep your mind off the business troubles. And maybe even gain a little perspective about what's really important.

In general, more breaks are better. As mentioned, when my kids were younger, I took generous amounts of time away with the family but made it clear to clients that I was available even while away. "If you can't bother me on vacation then I can't ever go," I used to tell them. Most never even knew I was away; I was doing whatever was necessary from the trip. Still better than not being able to go—and I was able to have some time to reflect and relax.

I had a client whose business was really booming. He was starting to feel the stress and knew if he went much longer things could really get out of hand in his psyche. With his wife's blessing he disappeared for two weeks to a mountain resort with no cell service. He checked e-mail once a day and only responded to the most urgent matters, leaving everything else to staffers. He biked, hiked, kayaked, and jet skied. He even met a new friend who became a close business colleague later.

Amazingly, the business survived. Customers were serviced, materials were ordered, products were shipped—everything was fine. He came back feeling a thousand times better, more energized, and happy. Of course, he also showed up with a yellow pad full of new thoughts and ideas to retool things to adjust to his unexpectedly booming business. He would not have had the time, or mindset, to think about that big picture if he was still stuck putting out fires all day.

For a female entrepreneur, that same mountain trip might do the trick. Or maybe a few days of spa life? A long weekend getaway with your spouse by the beach somewhere? Even a girls trip to some fun place can help recharge your batteries in a serious way. Two young female entrepreneurs I work with are overwhelmingly stressed from a variety of issues in their early-stage business. While they have had terrific success they are hard on themselves.

How do they manage the stress? I see them online pretty regularly talking about their girls' trip to Mexico, weekend in Las Vegas, and time by the beach on Long Island. You wouldn't know these ladies work like crazy when you see these postings, and of course they have to watch out for the "work hard/play hard" risks discussed earlier, but they tell me they are re-energized after these physical and mental vacations.

Part of this attempt at mental and emotional recharging can often include some time with a therapist. If you have had this experience, you have probably learned that therapy is neither the single solution to your problems nor an easy path. But it can be very helpful, especially in situations where you have real trouble seeing, as they say, the forest for the trees.

A good therapist will help you apply some logic and realism to a situation in which it is nearly impossible for you to be objective. This is not to suggest that therapists are or should be business consultants or personal business coaches, but they can help.

And what of radio legend Howard Stern? In 2010 he signed an additional five-year contract, even though he complained bitterly of being exhausted and not sure he could go on. His solution: Instead of the already-reduced four-day weekly schedule, he is now down to three days each week on the air. He is literally on the air about 12 hours per week to receive his untold millions. In fairness, we know he does much behind the scenes when he is not on the air.

Howard's version of take a break is to set up his life so that he is not working the majority of the time. Oh, and he takes plenty of vacation, as we pointed out earlier. In recent years, unfortunately, a pesky lawsuit between Stern and Sirius/XM over his compensation has also tapped his energy and desire to work for the company.

Will he sign on for another five years after this? The betting in Vegas is no. He may decide to continue his stint as a judge on *America's Got Talent*, or do other similar projects, but most believe he is ready to be done getting up at 4 AM.

Rely More on Others

In my prior firm, after 16 years of serving as managing partner, I handed the role to my cofounder and longtime friend. I found that I was not tired of practicing law, hustling for business, writing books, managing my practice team, traveling, and giving speeches. Moreover, I was still overseeing important decisions and policy matters, which is what I really cared about. But I was tired, after 16 years, of the daily grind of operating our multi-million-dollar business, and once I was no longer managing partner, I felt renewed energy towards the things I enjoy.

A good-sized client I had for years in the defense industry was led by a hardworking visionary who saw the company through, and then re-emerge from, a difficult bankruptcy. He eliminated most of their debt, issued a bunch of stock to the creditors, and kept going. A leaner and meaner operation quickly became profitable on about $30 million in revenues, and even started growing. But the CEO was getting close to that moment where he was beginning to worry about his enthusiasm and energy levels.

His longtime right hand, a financial type who served as chief financial officer, was well-liked in the company and had also been critical to the reorganization process. Unlike the CEO, while the CFO worked hard and of course worried about his job through the bankruptcy, he lived a balanced life, enjoying time with his wife, getting to the gym regularly, and not staying too late at work. His energy was terrific and, in fact, the emergence from bankruptcy made him even more determined to help the company really succeed.

My tired CEO decided, after discussions with his board, to let the CFO take over as CEO while our tired guy stayed with the title of president. They were both still full-time, but now the CFO was the one staying nights and worrying about everything. It was just what the now-former CEO needed to focus more on pursuing exciting new projects as he found some time away to think and plan. A year later the company was sold successfully.

As we discussed in Chapter 4, employing the "D" word (delegation) has its challenges, but it can be an essential tool in burnout prevention, and in treating burnout if it arrives. Here we are talking about literally handing some of your responsibilities permanently to one or more colleagues. This is not the same as asking subordinates to handle this or that project to let you go home a little earlier.

For husband and wife partners, rely more on each other. Most commonly one but not both partners is facing potential burnout. Allow yourself to depend a bit more on the spouse who still has some energy left. If spousal pressure is causing some of the burnout risk, both should work hard to be supportive of each other. Also, give each other space. If you are that rare couple that spends pretty much every waking minute together, it might be that perfect time for your spouse to take that golf or spa weekend, or let him or her have a bit more time with the kids—whatever works for you!

Do it yourself, or DIY, works great when you want to fix the gutters on your house or maybe put up some nice bookshelves. But as an entrepreneur, when you feel you are the only one who can handle certain things, chances are you are wrong. There are other capable people—if you followed our earlier advice and hired right! If you monitor their work, you can get a sense of whether you were wrong and adjust if necessary.

When Burnout Hits

Unfortunately, there are times when an entrepreneur's best-laid plans simply don't pan out as expected. You've tried to prevent exhaustion from even being an issue. And as signs of weariness crept in, you even went for some of the strategies previously described, but none enabled you to avoid the dreaded burnout. And you have a real sense that not much is going to change that.

The business is too slow. The business is too fast. Personal pressures overtake. Vacation won't help. Some delegation isn't changing anything.

Maybe you find yourself admitting that you are not actually cut out to be an entrepreneur (assuming you didn't have Chapter 2 to read beforehand!). You're just done.

This may well be the hardest moment for a one-time hard-charging entrepreneur to identify. The most objective advisor one has, unfortunately, is never oneself. If you are trying to come to a determination that you are done owning or at least running the business, you are asking if it is time to give up. You are probably the last one with any sort of clear head to make a decision of this import.

This goes against the entire spirit of what brought you to the freedom of entrepreneurship in the first place. Of course, much depends on the way in which you exit and what awaits you on the other side.

Some of the same strategies to try to prevent burnout in the first place could be employed to try to alleviate the symptoms when they hit. Change the plan, take a break, rely on others. You can and probably should try these before throwing in the towel.

So how do you decide? The reality is that only about half of U.S. startups are still in business five years after they start, and about 29 percent are left after 10 years (according to a July 15, 2009, *New York Times* article entitled "Failure Is a Constant in Entrepreneurship"). This is not unlike the marriage statistics, unfortunately. So if you have kept things going for a few years, you have already beaten the odds—and if you do decide to end the venture, you are by no means alone.

But there is this thing: You poured your soul into the business. You sacrificed everything, maybe invested your life savings. It became part of your identity to your friends, the world. You may not even admit it to yourself, but the business may feel about as important to you as one of your children. How can you abandon that?

Assuming you are giving up, before you do so make sure you answer another kind of important question: What are you going to do next? Some find themselves so burned out that they simply want out and have no thoughts or plan about the future. A big part of how you handle separating from the business will depend on what your next chapter will be.

Whether "coming next" includes some form of continuing with the business, we will analyze shortly. But if you are heading off to new pastures, are you planning on a regular executive job working for others? If you are in a service business, can you take some of your clients to a competitor and work there? What will that be like?

Let's add a few options to the table when it appears you simply cannot continue running the business due to sheer exhaustion and burnout.

Sell the Business

The CEO of a client with substantial revenues came to me after 20 years of building his business pretty much from nothing. Most were years of growth, but the last four years were rough, and revenues were up and down. Managing cash flow, meeting payroll—suddenly these were things he had to worry about for the first time since the very early years of the business.

Even though he had a good amount of money in the bank, he was not happy that he essentially gave up his bonus to make sure his people and vendors were paid. He would have preferred to ride the next 10 years successfully and then work out some sort of buyout arrangement with the company to allow him to retire while remaining chairman and maintaining a dignified relationship with the business.

But his energy was waning rapidly due to the four difficult years. He did his best to adjust his plan, but it was not easy to undo the infrastructure he had painstakingly built over such a long period. The last thing he wanted to do was send a message to employees that things were rough by starting layoffs. He worked harder to get and maintain new customers. Even though it was one of his great talents that helped build the business, it had been years since he personally made sales calls. But there he was, in a suit and tie (which he hated), doing his thing.

His industry was changing, but his business was synergistic with other larger companies that did not have the same capabilities. Over the years he had turned down a number of opportunities to sell the company, enjoying his freedom and control over his mini-empire, which he earned and deserved. Now, of course, things were different.

He watched his credit line, in so many years never accessed, not only being used but having to be increased. Suddenly the company was millions of dollars in debt in a very short time. The debt service was manageable, for now, because no principal was due for several years. But that clock was ticking, and he knew it.

The buzzards—sorry, I mean bankers—were circling and watching him carefully, making respectful but somewhat annoying suggestions about the business. He viewed this as interfering with his autonomy. (Why not sell this real estate that you've been holding for future expansion to raise some cash? Can you mechanize some functions to eliminate employees?) He did not like this.

He knew if he made an effort he would be able to pull through and get to the next upturn in business, but frankly he was utterly wiped out. He did not expect his late 50s to involve such stress and frustration. His wife was concerned, as he wasn't sleeping well, and seemed sad and worried all the time. He was in therapy, but it didn't seem to be doing much good.

His CFO, a longtime friend and ally, suggested they consider selling. "All our jobs will be saved," he said. My client could have a consulting arrangement but retire graciously, maybe even with a big payday. Even though the last few years had been rough in terms of cash flow, the paper profits of the business were not insignificant, and the debt, though an emotional burden, was a small percentage of the overall worth of the business.

Ultimately they found a buyer in a similar business that was able to absorb the business successfully. There were some layoffs, unfortunately, but all but one or two of the key executives remained. Our CEO indeed parachuted successfully into early retirement with an extremely nice eight-figure check. In the end he barely honored his one-year paid consulting arrangement, which was fine with the buyer.

Selling your business, if possible, is probably the most obvious way to address burnout. The advantages, of course, include the possibility of pulling some money out upon a sale. In addition, with a sale (versus shutting down; see following), most, if not all of your employees, will keep their jobs. As you move on to other things, your resume will hopefully read that you sold the business successfully and now it continues years later as a division of some other company.

A disadvantage is that the buyer may require you to stay and work for even up to three years, and this may make you doubly miserable. Not only will you have to continue in the business that burned you out, you will have to do so while working for someone else. Think carefully about this if the income from staying after a sale is important to you.

If you do want to stay and need to do so, make sure you don't win the battle and lose the war. Years ago I had a client in the telecommunications business ready to sell to a major company for a potential $28 million. The buyer, unfortunately, was insisting on all but $2.1 million of that price being dependent on future revenues from my client's exciting, but mostly unproven, product after the sale. Part of the deal also included the three original founders being employed by the major company. Frankly, they needed the money from working if all they were getting was $700,000 each up-front (after taxes, certainly not enough for them to retire on).

They also needed to work for the buyer to ensure that sales hit the levels they needed to in order to earn the remaining $25.9 million, obviously the big, important payday. But there was only one thing: The employment agreements were basically terminable by the buyer at six-month intervals. My clients figured they were safe and that no one could sell their product other than them.

They also felt the $2.1 million up-front was just plain unfair. They asked me to go back and demand that no deal is possible unless they paid $3 million, period. The buyer's counsel was very resistant—very annoyed to have this back and forth. Yes, for the buyer this was lunch money, but that was not the point. They prided themselves on making acquisitions that were extremely advantageous financially.

Ultimately, they relented and gave my clients the $3 million. We closed the deal. Six months later my clients were fired. I ran into the buyer's in-house counsel at a seminar. He said, "Those guys were dead on arrival. They should never have asked for that extra money up-front."

While it might not be your first choice, selling is a realistic option when you don't expect any relief from exhaustion. Just do it carefully.

Shut Down

A longtime client in an entertainment-related business decided that he was completely wiped out, after 15 years, of working constantly and building the business to about a $25 million-per-year level. He put in very long days, most weekends, constant travel, and fighting with his unions, for the most part successfully managing growth. Thankfully he was not a workaholic, but a super-determined and ambitious fellow.

But he did not know how to take breaks. He was too controlling to give up much power or responsibility. He made some, but not many, adjustments to his plan. Now, he was watching revenues plateau as his industry was consolidating.

He had put away about $10 million (pretty good for his early 40s!), but in the process, his marriage had ended over it. Luckily, he had found a new and more understanding girlfriend, whom he had met through business since he had no social life. He knew he was burned out and had to move on.

He first tried to sell the company. The only problem was, the one potential buyer changed his mind and decided not to go forward. Since no one was coming forward and he couldn't trust the business to anyone else, he thought for a bit. He already had what some would call "**** you" money and could retire, as he would say modestly, in his early 40s.

He made the tough decision to just close the doors. His next project: retirement, at least for a bit. (He came back later more on a project basis for things.) For those without $10 million, this may not be a viable option.

Shutting down is a difficult and possibly the most emotionally charged of the options upon burnout. To some it connotes failure. To others it's just downright embarrassing. Selling the company—that's a success no? Remember my radio station? How challenging it was for us? Our need to sell it for a loss? Yet some people read that I bought, owned, and then sold a radio station. I know it was not my greatest moment. You might not know that from reading the headlines. But if the headline was that I bought and then later shut down the business, there's only one interpretation.

Shutting down also can make sense in the down situation where payables and obligations are racking up, you don't see any possible way to make everyone whole, bankruptcy for whatever reason is not an option, and at least by ceasing operations you stop the bleeding. If you are shutting down in a situation like this, be careful to get good legal advice. In general, if you have structured your business as a corporation or limited liability company, you should avoid personal exposure for the debts and obligations of the business if you shut down. But, as mentioned, there are situations in which business owners agree to personally guarantee bank lines or other obligations.

In addition, aggressive creditors can try to argue that you are personally responsible even though an obligation was solely through the business. One way to do this is to attempt to "disregard the corporate entity." Others call it "piercing the corporate veil." This is not a legal treatise, and you need to get good legal advice. But in general if you have commingled personal and company funds, or not followed corporate formalities like issuing stock or holding board meetings, or are undercapitalized, creditors may have an argument to make you personally liable for things.

Also, note that some tax obligations may be subject to personal liability risk to those running the business even though incurred by the business. Make sure, if you are shutting down, that all your sales and payroll taxes are paid.

If you do go this route, don't despair! You took a chance that a small percentage of folks do. Maybe you were even successful for a bit. Maybe it's a time in the economy when tons of businesses are failing, in many cases through no real fault of their own. And just maybe you are like my client, and have actually cashed out a bit and have some decent savings for your effort. Even in arguable failure, you have succeeded—in going for it.

Hand It Over

More dramatic than simply relying on others, this option has you literally leaving the business and letting someone else run it. I am assuming, again, that you are simply too exhausted to continue. Maybe you can't let go completely, so sale or shutting down is not an option. Maybe you would like to sell but there are no buyers, and you have some personal guaranties that make shutting down difficult. Part of you may hope that one day you might return.

Try to analyze the pros and cons of handing over the reins versus other options from a financial point of view. This will not be easy since emotions are involved, but make the attempt. Maybe you can't handle a sale emotionally, but a buyer is prepared to wipe out your debt and hand you a check. In some circumstances this might be better than retaining the business' obligations and hoping that a third party will keep things going successfully.

There is the whole "legacy" aspect of dealing with a sale or shut down that hits many entrepreneurs in this situation. Those two options, in most cases, do not allow a founder to watch the continued success of his "child." Even in a sale, often the original business becomes unrecognizable a few years thereafter. This can frustrate selling entrepreneurs, who often are promised that nothing will change.

When you hand things over, the likelihood of a real legacy is greater. When I left the first law firm I cofounded after four years and modest growth, I was pleased to watch it continue to grow over the years. Today that firm, more than 20 years old, is still doing well. While my name is no longer on the door, maybe one day they'll put a portrait of my original partner and me with the caption "Our Founders" (just kidding, guys).

What does handing it over really mean? One choice is that you remain involved as chairperson. This is how Bill Gates at Microsoft ultimately promoted himself and let the day-to-day running of the business go to others while he focused on major strategic matters and his charitable endeavors. Alternatively, you can simply remain as a shareholder and advisor. The extreme version of hand it over is that you keep your shares but remain as a "silent partner," receiving regular reports but not planning on being involved at all or giving advice.

Which way to go depends on various factors. First is your emotional state. Are you beyond ready to be 100 percent free of hearing about things except when absolutely necessary or at specified intervals? Are you sure you can handle someone else making every important decision without you? Hopefully you can convince yourself that this beats shutting down or selling to someone who will destroy your legacy.

The next factor to consider is what your next step is. Are you planning to live off whatever profits come from the business? Maybe stay home and take care of the kids? Are you going back to a regular salaried position? Are you thinking of starting something else new? In general, the busier you are likely to be, the more you will be able to handle the handover. If you have no kids and plan to sit around the house waiting for checks, this is unlikely to be healthy for you.

The last, and by no means least, thing to think about in considering a handover is this: Who are you handing things over to? Suffice it to say that the more competent and motivated the person who will be in charge, the more content you are likely to be with the situation. That doesn't mean he or she will do things as you want, and it certainly does not guarantee success.

While you want the business to thrive after you, accept that there will be part of you that wants the successor to fail just to show the world that only you could build and run the business. Try to get to that place where you realize what is true: If the successor succeeds, it is much more likely to make you look good than the opposite.

The handover technique is particularly common to family businesses. Selling a family business can be difficult, and often many mouths are being fed by the profits the business generates, so shutting down is very much to be avoided. When the founder hits exhaustion, passing the torch to the next generation makes sense.

It does tend to be hard when the original founder first has to hand things over to his or her own children, but hopefully he or she is smart enough to know when it is time, not only for the founder's own psyche, but for his or her children's well-being, to let them take over. The handoffs to generations after that will, for good or bad, likely mirror the process taken by the founder, so think carefully about the precedent you are setting.

Therefore . . .

My 11-year-old son's comment in reading the title of this chapter: "Ha . . . you said poop."

I hope the most important message you took from this chapter is that burnout can be prevented most of the time. Run the marathon, not the sprint. Give yourself a chance for perspective. Adjust to changes in reality. Business is not easy; accept that. Not every moment will feel like those first few months of freedom. But don't forget to appreciate achievements when they happen.

You are more likely to avoid or manage burnout when the company is flying high than when it is struggling. This is not to downplay weariness that comes from too much success, as having more orders than you can accept is a real problem.

Also, a theme throughout here: Use your advisors when key decision moments are upon you. Your counsel, accountant, consultant, therapist, spouse, and key employees all can have useful and wise input as you ponder things.

But much like a U.S. president, who is only consulted on things his key staff cannot agree upon, you may face differing views from various well-intentioned folks. Do what you can to sift through the advice and then do your entrepreneur best to roll the dice whichever way when you are just "too pooped to produce."

CHAPTER 9

Battling Boredom in a Growing Company

How could a hard-driving entrepreneur ever get bored? Presumably one of the main reasons you started your own business was to jump out of bed every morning and look forward to the challenges of the day ahead. But what if you suddenly find yourself dreading going in to work from the sheer unexcitingness of it?

Boredom is different from burnout, which occurs from simple exhaustion. Here, you may not be tired, but the business may have gotten to a point where your focus goes elsewhere. You have simply reached a place where you are no longer interested in the business.

After many years working his way up to a senior executive position in a company, a friend—let's call him Henry—managed to get a nice payday when the company was sold. So he decided to take part of those proceeds to finally have a chance to do something on his own. He settled on buying a shipping business. It was already profitable and successful, with a steady group of customers. The first few years were exciting, as he dove into the details of the business, making some positive changes.

Having been an executive all his life, Henry was enjoying the freedom of controlling his destiny. And by buying in at a later stage, he avoided the hassle of building something from scratch. From the beginning the business not only remained profitable, but new customers continued to come, not at an unbearable pace, and it was frankly through little effort since almost all the new customers were simply referred by existing ones. It's the best way to get business!

He took over a terrific team of senior executives who really knew their stuff. The sales manager had great relationships with the customers, and his warehouse and operations staff were crackerjack and dealt with whatever issues arose, whether it was a truck needing repair or an issue with a supplier supposedly sending stuff to be shipped.

Truthfully, few problems made their way up the ladder to him. When one longtime executive retired, his successor was not only being groomed but had also been there over 10 years. Within four years Henry made enough to earn back his purchase price, in addition to taking a reasonable salary for himself. Things could not be going better. He exceeded his plans, and was living well with his wife and four kids. His staff seemed content with the way he was treating and compensating them. So why complain?

He did complain. Of sheer boredom. He didn't feel needed. Sure, he had regular meetings with the senior team, but virtually every major decision was handed to him by the key staff, and he rarely disagreed.

I asked Henry why he was so bored. He said, "The customers are solid. The team is terrific. The trucks come in and the trucks go out and I get money. There's really nothing for me to do."

One big challenge anyone faces when boredom sets in is what I call the "waa waa" problem. Many look at a successful business and wonder why anyone would be upset when they make a lot of money and simply lose interest in it. Just go in and do nothing, they would say; we all wish we could do that! So, these misunderstanding folks think, "Who would cry for a bored but successful entrepreneur?" But this can be a serious problem. If it does hit you, however, consider limiting who you talk to about it so that you avoid being labeled a complainer.

In this chapter, we will talk more about what Henry did to deal with his ennui, as well as other ideas for avoiding and dealing with boredom. Let's turn first to where it all comes from.

Causes of Boredom

Henry showed us one of the causes of boredom. The "smooth as silk" path that is so rare in business, if it continues, can easily cause an entrepreneur to lose focus since, frankly, there isn't much in the way of challenge. In general, boredom comes only when a business is very successful, or otherwise profitable and stable. If your business is struggling, or facing some difficulty, you are extremely likely to be heavily engaged in dealing with it, and you will not have the choice to be inattentive or uninterested.

In my decades of practice I have seen three major causes of boredom: too much growth, too much delegation, and a bad fit between the entrepreneur and his choice of business.

Too Much Growth

Too much growth is a good problem. Suddenly you find yourself at the helm of a company doing $100 million in sales when just a few years ago you had $20 million in sales and a few key executives. Or maybe things get even bigger; maybe you have completed some acquisitions that have brought rapid growth to the size of the business.

One would think this would be the dream scenario for an entrepreneur. There are some, as we will discuss, who do remain motivated and interested even as the business grows phenomenally. But for many, there is that point, when it gets harder to really call the business "entrepreneurial," at which point boredom begins to set in.

What happens when a business grows? More management is needed. I have often told clients that the risk of a founder's boredom increases directly with the increase in the size of a company's middle management. What happens when that extra layer of executives arrives? Meetings. Reports. Committees. The need for consensus. Office politics. Isn't avoiding all this part of why most entrepreneurs leave the big company life in the first place?

Those who live with an entrepreneurial streak simply chafe in that world of careful planning and endless discussion.

Too Much Delegation

Another cause of boredom is an excess of delegation. Yes, we preach here the importance of giving as much as you can to capable employees so that you can focus more on the very high-level stuff. But what if there isn't that much to focus on? My friend Henry watched the business grow steadily but manageably, watched his terrific executives handle things, and occasionally has to weigh in on things like getting a new truck or some issue with a low-level employee.

Now, sure, a driven entrepreneur in Henry's shoes might say, "With all my free time, I have to shake things up. Maybe I'll buy another business. Maybe I will expand with other shipping locations. Let me think of things to speed growth even more." But Henry was doing well, living well, and saving for retirement, but he really didn't have other money on top of that for most of the things mentioned.

A client of mine on the West Coast is a copper distributor, and his wife is his partner. His father and uncle had started the company, and then allowed him (and her) to take over when they retired. Like my friend Henry, this client has an awesome team, some of whom have been with the company for decades. The business generates millions in revenues and a high-six-figure income for the couple.

In this case the hard-driving one is his wife. He is also entrepreneurial and appreciates the freedom they have running their own business. But with his wife running things, he finds he just doesn't have much to do all day. He walks around the warehouse, keeps an eye on expenses, and occasionally needs to sit with his bank to renew their credit line, but that's really about it. Yet he gets up every day and goes to work with his wife.

This client told me he is going crazy from boredom. His wife is busy getting new customers, overseeing the operations and staff, and, yes, from time to time consulting with him about important decisions. He's more than thrilled with how she handles things and supports her 100 percent. And she seems to enjoy the challenge of being in charge.

Like Henry, their risk capital is already in the business, and they don't have spare cash, despite living well, to take more risk like an acquisition. So my friend just watches his wife run things beautifully.

Interestingly, at home they have much different roles. They are traditional people: She cooks dinner and does laundry; he shovels snow and fixes things around the house. They make all decisions regarding their children together. They have succeeded, for the most part, in keeping business talk out of the house. In fact, they are a happy couple.

But he is still frustrated at work. He doesn't want to speak to her about it because the delicate balance they have worked out is good for the business, which is good for their family. Later in the chapter we'll cover some options for him. (He is still in the business, and nothing has changed.)

Wrong Business

When you start a business presumably you have determined that there is no question that you are right for that type of business and you will be excited about building a company in that field. What if that turns out to be wrong?

I had a client a number of years ago in the real estate business in South Florida. During the 2000s he did phenomenally well. He started in the business as a salesman in another company because he wanted a chance to make a lot of money, and he did—enough to start and build his own company.

Somewhere around 2005 he had an epiphany: He actually hated the real estate business! He liked the money he was making, but he found so many things about the industry annoying, difficult, or frankly sleazy. He was constantly dealing with crooked guys who wanted to work with or help him. Most seemed genuine and legitimate until he checked them out and learned bad things about their backgrounds. He felt like he wanted to do something more meaningful than moving money around.

As a result, he started dreading going to work. The business still ran fine, but he was less and less interested in it. The business just kept growing whether he showed up for work or not, but he kept showing up. He was only 38 years old, certainly not ready to retire! How did he ultimately handle this? We'll see soon.

How many entrepreneurs, as children, thought they would be running a company like the one they founded? For some, they wake up and discover that they are just in the wrong business. (For the record, at age 9, I wanted to be an astronaut.)

In many cases people found companies in the industry in which they grew up. Often people fall into a field almost by accident. You went on 30 job interviews and this was the one that offered. Next thing you know, you have 10 years under your belt and take a shot at doing it on your own. But do you really love it? Or do you go into it just because it's what you know?

I'm lucky to enjoy what I do as an attorney. I get to use my brain every day, something my friend Henry told me he envies while he's sitting around his shipping company office. I love the challenge of structuring transactions, the fun of watching companies grow, and the thrust and parry of negotiation. And of course I enjoy working with my terrific team as well as my writing, traveling, and speaking engagements.

But I never dreamed of being a lawyer. My traditional Jewish parents told me I could be anything I want, but before that I had to finish my education with a "profession." To them that was law, medicine, accounting, and maybe engineering. How did I settle on law? My dad was a surgeon, but early on I learned that blood and I are not a good combination. When I took my first accounting course at Wharton I knew pretty quickly that was not for me. Engineering? Nope. I was never into that technical stuff. So law it was. I got a great summer job in a Manhattan law firm after my second year of law school, and the rest is history.

As I have described, I was not happy with large law firm life, and thought about getting out of law and into finance. I stuck with it when people talked me out of it. But since I had "fallen" into law, it seemed logical to deal with my unhappiness by starting my own firm. And yes, it worked out well and I am the furthest thing from bored, but others are not so lucky.

Preventing or Overcoming Boredom

There are some similarities and some stark differences between the options for dealing with boredom and burnout. As we will cover, selling the business, leaving someone else in charge, and just shutting down are certainly ways to deal with your ennui.

But some of the burnout remedies don't work here. If you take a break, which helps in exhaustion cases, you still come back to your unhappiness at work. Adjusting your plan also doesn't really apply. As discussed, boredom is most likely to hit when things are going great and there's no need to adjust the plan.

How is it that super-successful billionaires like Bill Gates and the late Steve Jobs started companies from scratch and for the longest time continued to run them, seemingly happily, even after they became huge companies? We return to my hero Howard Stern as well. He's got quite the operation that reportedly has $100 million a year in costs. How does he deal with the added layers of folks sitting at this part of his journey when not long ago there was a staff of three or four?

And what of sad Henry, and my real estate client and my copper distributor? Here's how to deal with boredom.

Sell, Leave, or Shut Down

When you find that you are no longer interested in your business, it may well be time to disengage from it. As with burnout, if you found that the bigger company life, way-too-capable lieutenants, or the very industry you are in are taking away your focus, getting out may make sense.

That's what my real estate guy did. In 2007, right before the mortgage and real estate meltdown (he later admitted this was just dumb luck), he sold his company to a much larger business doing the same thing. Before taxes he got to keep about $25 million. Unlike the challenges in a burnout situation, which include the sadness of letting go a "child," my client really did come to hate his business. He was actually glad to see it go.

But, as mentioned, he was 38 and didn't want to retire. His wife was a practicing attorney who enjoyed her job and didn't want to quit, so it's not like the two of them could travel the world and enjoy life. He certainly didn't want to stay home with the kids; he adored them but knew he wasn't built for 24/7 babysitting.

He got his chance at a longtime dream. My client took about 10 percent of the net money he made (around $1 million) and helped found an exciting software company. This client had always been very into technology. In fact, he helped write some unique software that his real estate company had utilized and actually licensed to others.

Unfortunately, the new dream didn't work out so well. He was unsuccessful in raising more money for the company and did not want to risk more of his nest egg earned from the sale of the real estate business. So he got, as we say, a nice write-off when he had to shut the company two years after it started.

But in the experience something important happened. He wasn't bored in the new company. He was so excited every day to work with the team he put together. He was truly disappointed when it didn't work out. So even though he lost his investment, he had fun trying, and luckily he was in a financial position to absorb the loss.

When I last checked in with him, he was making some smaller investments, in the $100,000 range, in early-stage companies—a true angel. He realized, after his multiple forays into entrepreneurship, he had much to offer young startups in addition to just his money. He provided advice, on what helped him succeed, but also what he learned from his failures.

Again, he's not bored. While he's not operating a company anymore, he loves the freedom to spend time with his investments at his convenience, but not have to dive in as intensely as he did with his own businesses. He has more time with the family, which he enjoys, and his wife has even cut back her hours so they can do more together. Nice happy ending, and it all started with boredom!

But be careful when a possible sale is coming. One of the risks of boredom is that the business does in fact require your touch, and your disengagement leads to complacency. One client of mine who got frustrated with how much his company had started resembling the big places he always hated spent most of his office time playing video games on his office computer.

This went on for several years. During that brief time, many changes came to his industry, and his ability to compete was more and more difficult. His revenues and profits began to shrink, and when he sold, he got a lot less than he would have if he had kept his focus and reacted to the changes in his industry.

As with burnout, shutting down is also an option if you're bored. Again you have to see what your financial ability to handle things is. In this context, you are shutting down a presumably successful and thriving business, so hopefully you are financially set enough to give up what one assumes is a nice living.

What's more, with shutting down, as mentioned in Chapter 8, your employees also lose their jobs. Does that really make sense if the business is doing well? When my real estate guy sold, only 10 percent of his employees were let go. That beats firing everyone.

What could work better than shutting down is the option to hand over the keys to a top executive and stay as an uninvolved shareholder. If the business was doing well with you bored, there's hopefully a decent chance that it will remain successful and you can move on to whatever is next.

For old Henry, well, he kind of did that. He started going to the office only two or three days a week, and spending the rest of his time on his boat fishing. He's been doing that now for about three years, and I've never seen him happier. The business remains successful, and he's less bored when he's only there a little bit because the few things he has to handle get crammed into less time.

Check Your Personality

Now back to Gates, Jobs, and Stern as we talk about checking your personality. Some folks just happen to have the right personality to avoid boredom even as their enterprises grow rapidly. If you are starting a business that has a chance to grow to be large, think carefully about whether you are the type of person who might enjoy or even thrive in a company at every stage from startup to very large indeed.

One such personality type tends to occupy what I like to call the "size matters" school of entrepreneurship. Leaders like Sanford (Sandy) Weill, who ran Citigroup for years after a successful history on Wall Street, exemplify this type. It's all about how to make things bigger. Sandy seemed to live for the next deal that would grow his empire more. What got him going? Focusing on that deal. Is some of it probably ego-based? Yes.

Another legend who seems to fit this deal-focused, "bigger is better" category is real estate mogul Donald Trump. In fact Trump wrote a book called *The Art of the Deal*, in which he provides tips from the many transactions he has been part of. Trump is famous for arguing with anyone who claims to be able to calculate his net worth. He was said to be worth $7 billion in 2011 when he was seriously considering running for president. In 2005 he sued a *New York Times* reporter who suggested his net worth may only be about $250 million. Yes, Donald, size matters.

So as big as things get for Donald, who has built, busted, and rebuilt his business, he remains driven to keep building and buying. He started with about 27,000 apartments that his father owned (their family name was Drumpf before they emigrated and changed it) and just couldn't stop. Whatever your thoughts on The Donald, you must respect his tenacity, focus, and success.

In many ways this approach requires someone who is the ultimate macromanager. You can be in charge of your large and growing company, but leave all but the largest decisions to others, and spend your day looking for ways to grow the business. Maybe that means seeking organic growth, but more commonly this happens through acquisitions.

If you enjoy that ride, boredom will not be your problem. The drive to be bigger and buy things can literally be never-ending. Weill's career saw a series of involvement with companies that grew and grew by swallowing up others.

And what of the richest man in the world, Bill Gates? In the latest *Forbes* list of the 400 wealthiest people in the world, Gates is listed as having $66 billion. Not bad for a college dropout (okay, yes, it was Harvard) who built a computer in the garage. How did Bill stay involved and engaged when his company was the largest in the world?

Bill is a bit control-focused. Let's not call him a control freak as we discussed in earlier chapters. But those who know him say that he has a visceral need to control everything in his world. If he can't control it he has to crush it. It sounds harsh, but hey it's business. I think to this day it drives him nuts that he was not able to make his arch-rival Apple go away.

What kept Bill going was the challenge of taking on the next competitor, supplier, or vendor that was not pleasing him. There were various lawsuits, in which Microsoft ultimately paid out money, where they were accused of putting hidden features in their computer operating systems that made it harder or even impossible to use certain competitors' software products on the system—even though Microsoft's whole strategy in marketing its operating systems was to be the honest platform on which anything would work.

And it appears that shock jock Stern stayed focused as his business became rather substantial because of a very simple mantra: He could not rest until every single person in America (and now the world) is listening to him and only him on the radio.

Stern claims he visits his psychiatrist three to four times a week to deal with issues such as this. It does appear he has softened his competitive nature as his net worth has grown and, possibly, because he has had good therapy. Indeed even his choice to move to satellite was with the knowledge that his total audience was likely to shrink dramatically. (As discussed it was more about the money and the freedom to continue uncensored.)

Before all this, Stern effectively innovated the idea of simulcasting his live morning drive broadcast in multiple cities through syndication. As he entered some cities and then rapidly crushed the competition, he would go there and stage a "funeral" for the previous market leading DJ. He would call their shows, belittling them and their talents.

Poor John Debella in Philadelphia. He was the first that Howard defeated in the late 1980s. Debella, a very popular DJ on the top-40 station there, for years led a parade in Philly, singing the famous song "Louie Louie" all the way. Well, Howard, who made fun of Debella for being bald, wrote a parody of that song called "Baldy Baldy," came to Philadelphia, and sang it in front of Debella's radio station studio building at his "funeral."

Then it was on to the next city, and the next, and so on. And then taking on satellite, where he dreamed of dominating an exciting, relatively new technology. Unfortunately Sirius/XM has not fared entirely as hoped and its stock is a perennial underachiever. In fact, as mentioned Stern is currently in litigation with his employer, disagreeing with its interpretation of what he was supposed to earn in his first five-year contract.

So Howard, as mentioned in Chapter 8, may have been challenged by burnout, but I don't think he's ever been bored.

And the late great Steve Jobs of Apple? It was simple there: He loved the process of innovation. Even as his company grew and grew, he was very involved in all aspects of developing new products. Jobs's recent biography includes a description of the lab in which new products are developed. Apparently Jobs visited the lab quite often when he wasn't ill.

Jobs was big into how products looked and felt more than he was focused on all the whizbang technology inside. He also thought about each new product in context to the company's entire product line and strategy. He managed to think big and small at the same time.

His fun was developing something new and getting it out there. So even though, like Gates, he started the company from scratch, he remained focused and interested even as it became huge (of course, for very different reasons than Gates, but nonetheless). Indeed, maybe our friend Bill could have learned a thing or two from Jobs. Some of Microsoft's best-known failures were failures of technology. In fairness, Apple had its rough periods as well.

So if you are lucky enough to have great interest and focus on one area of your business and like to dive into it, you may have a much greater chance to avoid boredom in your successful company.

Re-Engage

Another treatment for boredom is to re-engage in some aspect of the business. There is no business that is run perfectly. There are always things that can be improved. You may not have Jobs's love of one part of the business, but consider picking something anyway. Maybe you'll be more involved in a new hire or a new product line. Maybe lead an examination into something the business is doing to see if improvement is possible. Create what is hopefully a worthwhile project for yourself.

In other words, get back your focus. What will be interesting to you? Presumably you know best. Even if capable people are running the area you will focus on, and they may not love what they might consider to be interference, do it anyway. Try to convey that they should consider it a compliment that you want to focus efforts on working with them to make their area even more important.

There are other ways to re-engage. Maybe try to eliminate some of the red tape that has developed in your organization and leading in part to your disinterest. In the classic movie *Big*, the head of fictional McMillan Toys, Mr. McMillan, expresses frustration with how the fun has gone out of his business. He visits toy stores to see how real people are buying. He says to Josh Baskin, a kid who has magically transformed into looking like an adult, "You can't see this on a marketing report." Josh innocently replies, "What's a marketing report?" Says McMillan, "Exactly."

Clearly poor Mr. McMillan was frustrated with the bureaucracy he had built. He hires Baskin to think up new toys that didn't come out of spreadsheets and market studies. Their simple rule is that a toy has to be fun. After McMillan shakes things up in his company, he declares: "I'm having fun again."

Not out of boredom, but necessity, when corporate profits improve near the end of most recessions, much of that improvement is due to cost-cutting rather than revenue growth. This is one of the reasons that, in general, corporate profits tend to improve coming out of recessions before the unemployment figures do.

Managing costs is not something that should wait for a recession. It is a natural tendency to be less focused on costs when profits are strong or even growing. But of course that feeling should be resisted. Any business can always benefit from a fresh look at how the business is run and whether all costs are necessary.

As discussed earlier, you may want to think about the impact on morale if letting people go could be part of the strategy. That's part of what you can decide to focus on. Shaking things up in a healthy and careful way does not have to be a bad thing. And now, for the first time, you would have the luxury of time to actually be careful.

Not that you want a million meetings on the subject—that's exactly what you're trying to eliminate—but one way to regain focus is to look at your overhead and tighten things up.

I have also seen a few bored entrepreneurs step out. By that I mean, start, resume, or increase your business networking. You may have done that for years but you lost touch in the early years of the business when that was your whole focus. In pretty much every industry there are conferences, meetings, and gatherings of players.

Chances are if you are successful you might even be sought after as a speaker. Or spend a few bucks and sponsor a few events, bringing visibility to the business. Building (or rebuilding) a network is a great way to bring back attention and focus. A good friend of mine is a master networker who has written books on the subject. I think I'm pretty good at it, but to watch this guy work a room is like watching Yo-Yo Ma on his Stradivarius. He spends hours on follow-up.

The key to building a network, to me, is to make it the process of making friends. What better way to re-engage in your business? Go out there, talk about your success, make friends, and then help each other where you can. Even talk to your competitors. There are usually things in common that you can relate to. Is there some pending legislation that will hurt your whole industry? Maybe work with them on that. Make friends.

Another way to re-engage is to do some high-level strategic planning. I served on a not-for-profit board for a number of years. Some of those years were very difficult for the charity, where it really struggled to pay its costs, and luckily several major benefactors kept things going. But they were in true survival mode for quite a while. Then, things got much better over a period of about three years. Finally we began to breathe collective sighs of relief.

We then realized that it had been quite a long time since we had engaged in any long-term planning. The charity's space was changing, and it had to adapt, but no one had the time to do anything but survive. Finally, with things in better shape, the board meetings included reports from a newly created strategic planning committee. The whole board did a two-day retreat with professional facilitators to really get the ideas flowing. It was terrific.

While this is neither a boredom nor burnout story, it is similar in that an entrepreneur's road to boredom comes from being overwhelmed by how the business has grown or the other factors described. So what better way to use time you've now forced onto yourself than to think about the long term?

Strategic long-term planning is often disregarded in the crazy life of an entrepreneur. As mentioned earlier in our discussion of financing, it is nearly impossible to predict what the next few years will bring to a young or growing business. Plan anyway! You can posit multiple scenarios and play out what you might do in response. Or find a good likely conservative path and plan that way.

Spend time studying your industry. What can you learn from your competitors? Are things changing at all? Ask where you would really like the business to be in three to five years financially. Then ask what different possible scenarios could get you there. If you can afford it, bring in a consultant to help. Good ones can be really good.

Spend some time brainstorming with your team. Put sticky notes all over a board, think big, think innovative, but think practical. They will appreciate being involved and hopefully bring some good ideas.

The last thing to consider as a step toward re-engagement is to bring in a business coach. A coach is different from a consultant, who focuses on how to make the business better. A coach will help you make yourself better for the business. A big difference!

I have used one and found it tremendously helpful in dealing with issues I faced for a long time. For example, I am not great at time management. I would say yes to too many people and things, and too often would end up running late or struggling to meet deadlines. My coach really worked with me to significantly improve my management skills in this area.

For a bored company founder, a coach might be just what you need. A coach can, obviously, go much deeper into your situation than the few pages of this chapter to take a look at what caused your boredom and spend time with you exploring different paths to treating it.

Therefore . . .

As we close this last substantive chapter before concluding the book, know that I consider boredom one of the greatest risks a growing business faces. I have seen too many times where it means the end of a business, and as discussed, it does not always need to be that way.

From Henry to my real estate guy to Gates and Stern, we now realize to look for the signs that could lead to losing focus, and some ways to address boredom if it does show up. Advice: Don't plan to get big, unless your personality is right for it, or unless you're ready to sell or give up control when ennui hits. Don't delegate too much or you can delegate yourself right out of a challenge.

And pick the right business, for goodness sake. Take your time before you make that big decision to dive into entrepreneurship, and make sure you are right for the business you have chosen. The business should bring you freedom, not a proverbial albatross around your neck.

CHAPTER 10

The Greatest Challenges

If you have made it this far, congratulations! Hopefully you have completed your self-analysis to determine if you have enough of the personality traits of a successful entrepreneur. If you have already started a business, you've probably already thought about the right ways to make the perfect matches with your partners, employees, and financing. You have taken the "work/less work" challenge head on and done your best to address it. You worked hard to prevent or at least treat boredom and burnout. And you made sure not to lose focus on your business even when great new ideas come along.

Actually, in my more than 20 years of working with entrepreneurs, I have never met one who got everything exactly right. To conclude, we will talk a bit about where the greatest challenges really lie, and where more people rise to the occasion on these issues which most entrepreneurs face.

Then we finish off with a look at someone close to me who shows us so many of the right ways to do things: my uncle, Leonard Rivkin.

Failures in any of the areas covered in this book can be significant or even deadly, and in no way do I wish to downplay the importance of them all. However, if pressed, I believe the three most common reasons entrepreneurial ventures fail are (1) lack of capital, (2) bad partner choices, and (3) personality traits that lead to burnout or loss of focus. Let's cover each.

Insufficient Capital

So many resources one encounters on new companies lament that a large number of businesses fail due to undercapitalization. My second venture into entrepreneurship (my radio station) clearly didn't make it for that reason. Why does this happen so often? Most founders plan carefully and conservatively, and yet still things don't seem to go as planned. Or there was an expectation that funds could be raised on an ongoing basis and it turns out that was not the case.

So many early-stage companies have an ongoing need to raise money to keep going. Of course, they all hope to get to that point where they are self-sufficient. But even when that happens, there can be bumps along the way where cash flow becomes a major problem. How much of a reserve you have, and how you manage your overhead, all play into your ability to weather a downturn.

In our earlier discussion about finding the right investor, we talked a bit about the importance of aligning with someone who can continue to be there to provide capital on an ongoing basis. Your friends and family, while an attractive source (especially in the early stages), are not likely to provide multiple rounds of financing. Venture, private equity, and PIPE investors are more likely, but as discussed, come with more restrictions on your activities.

The goal, as we touched on, is to combine careful planning with finding the right investors. As we discussed earlier, when things are going well, try to build a decent store of cash. Don't hire that extra person just yet, or make a commitment to additional space or warehouse until you really have to. Also, don't wait too long to adjust your overhead if business is turning down. These are the keys to managing cash flow.

I served on a board of a charity on which there was tremendous attention paid to the annual budget. The budget was set up on an accrual basis. This meant that, for example, interest accruing on debt but not being paid counted as an expense. It also meant that some of the charity's operations, which had different seasons, were counted looking backward in the budget rather than forward. In addition, other non-cash expenses such as depreciation were included.

Expenses that were deemed capital expenditures rather than routine expenses were amortized over a period of years. So, a $35,000 purchase of equipment only showed up in the budget as $7,000 each year for five years, but the $35,000 expense was paid now.

I watched various executives with profit-and-loss control over their aspects of the charity manipulate this. They would think, "I can buy this because only one-fifth shows up this year, and the budget won't look so bad. They will just have to find the cash; that is secondary."

None of this seemed to matter in reality for the charity, which generated millions in revenues each year. The budget looked nice for the accountants, but was a relatively useless guide for how to manage the charity's finances.

Most entrepreneurs I know feel similarly. I certainly did when I ran a law firm with millions in revenues. All I cared about was the cash flow report and the budget based on cash. We didn't even bother with an accrual-based budget. Cash, indeed, is king.

An accrual-based budget can matter, for example, in a public company that will be reporting its results to the world in accrual form. Did we make money or lose money? The legitimate gimmickry that sometimes accompanies the preparation of those, frankly, at times belies providing real insight into a company's actual financial position.

This discussion is important because obtaining the right reports of how your business is doing is critical. Even a good accounting software cash report can tell you much, assuming you avoid the "garbage in-garbage out" risk of humans entering data.

Do your best to avoid undercapitalization and be strategic about how you raise money. If you determine that you will need $1.5 million to get through the next 12 months, ask yourself how sure you are that this is the right amount. If you could raise more, would you?

Of course, don't go crazy, because raising too much may not be ideal either. If you plan for the value of your company to continue to rise, then you need to find the right balance between safety and dilution.

The more you raise earlier and at a lower value, the more your interest in the company will be reduced. You'd rather sell $1.5 million of stock two years from now when the company is worth $10 million than $1.5 million of stock now when the company is worth $5 million.

Bad Partner Choices

Just as there are tons of books on how to make your personal long-term relationships and marriage work or work better, there really should be a book on how to get along with and solve problems with your business partner.

What are some of the many difficulties that are more likely to be deadly for a business? The biggest is misunderstandings going in. *I thought I was going to be the "senior" partner with the other one mostly deferring to me. I thought my partner had tremendous capability in key areas that it turns out she does not. I thought we were going to split up day-to-day responsibilities equally. I thought we were going to make all decisions jointly.* You name it.

Changed circumstances relating to your partner also can play a major role. *My business partner and I were a romantic couple and now we've split up. My partner is getting divorced and he is running around burning the candle at both ends and not as committed to the business. My partner controls our most important client and is trying to gain leverage on me with that. My partner has worked too hard and is now burned out. I brought in a much older partner who now wants to slow down.*

Last, changes in the business can have an impact. *My partner's lifestyle has always been bigger than mine, and now that there's a business slowdown it's created tremendous tension between us. We have adjusted our business model so that the areas of his strength are now much less important to the success of the business.*

Here's another very common one: He or she was important to the start of the business since I could not afford to pay someone to do what this person does, but now we have the money and I am resentful giving him or her a large percentage of profits forever to perform a function I could now easily hire someone to do.

Many romantic couples go to couples therapy. Maybe business partners should, too. The closest we have is to bring in a business coach. Some are willing to work with more than one "client" at a time. It is not a bad idea even if you just want to address these issues better, when problems arise, or frankly even before. But without therapy, what are some of the common methods I have seen people use to deal with partner problems?

First, as discussed earlier, be clear up-front. You can get so excited about a new business with a partner. Much like a new romantic relationship, you don't want to create any issues or spoil the "courtship" stage. There are concerns or issues you would like to raise but you decide not to. A new boyfriend leaving his socks on the floor starts out cute, then gets annoying.

Deciding not to raise these issues before committing to each other is almost definitely a mistake. As mentioned earlier, if you have problems going in, that is a bad sign. Let's say you have 10 years more experience than your partner. Even though you may have agreed to a 50/50 split of profits, you never really discussed how the business is to be managed. You assume it's you at the helm and your partner assisting. He or she may well assume otherwise. Get this straight up-front.

Since you are taking my advice and having a written agreement with your partner, during that process is the time to work out things that could become problems later. Don't just hope your partner gets it and can read your mind.

Have a clear understanding of who is going to do what in the business. If you are bringing in someone because of specific talents or capabilities, if you have not already done so, do what is necessary to test and ensure he or she really has the skill. Better that he or she feels a little offended up-front than to discover you brought in the wrong person when it is too late.

One of the most important aspects of this agreement with your partner is making sure it includes a way to exit the arrangement if irreconcilable differences develop. As we discussed, buy-sell and other similar provisions in an agreement can help make "corporate divorce" a bit less harrowing if it comes to that.

What should you do when your partner's situation changes for some reason? As with advice when business turns down leading to burnout, be prepared to adjust the plan. Does your older partner want to slow down? That might be okay if he or she agrees to adjust what each of you takes from the business. Or you can decide that your partner contributed sufficiently over the years to continue to be entitled to a full share.

This is also something that can be dealt with up-front, especially if you are starting with a much more experienced partner who, sooner rather than later, might want to be less committed. It is common with law firms, for example, to have withdrawal as a partner by a certain age with a predetermined buyout arrangement. You still might remain working at the firm, just no longer as a partner.

Is your partner getting divorced? Try to refocus him or her on the business. Maybe do the coach thing. Also keep in mind that short-term personal issues are almost guaranteed eventually to invade in any long-term business partnership. Do your best to be patient and understanding since it is just as likely to be you as your partner. In a few months, your divorcing partner may end up in a new relationship and calm down.

The same is true for a partner with a health issue or a new baby. These can take someone away from the business for a few months, but many come back with as much health and vigor as before (in some cases, more).

Some of these changes, however, could be permanent. Reconsider my friend who gave up his entrepreneurial venture because of his time commitment to his disabled son. Now imagine that this is your partner first discovering the issue several years into partnership with you. Here you may need to consider, if the partner is to continue with you, whether an adjustment in your deal makes sense because of his reduced time commitment.

Another client of mine was diagnosed with a serious disease. It is not curable and can ultimately be deadly, but many manage to be treated and can keep it under control for years—even decades—with only minimal symptoms. Or he may end up hospitalized repeatedly. You just cannot predict.

The normal "disability" provisions in partnership agreements tend to require you to be unable to perform for many months in a row or a number of months in a year before your partner has a right to ask you to leave and buy you out. The two partners of my client with the disease really struggled with how to handle this. What if you have a congenital problem that falls short of triggering the buyout but does noticeably interfere with your partner's ability to contribute?

It is best to sit down with your partner in that situation and talk things through. You do not want to wait until the situation becomes acute to address it. And of course you want to be as supportive as you can when the partner is going through something difficult. Hopefully your partner, if he or she is honest with himself or herself, would understand that you need to do what is best for the business.

This does not mean that any change in your arrangement is mandated. Remember working hard versus working smart? If your partner with the ill child is responsible for sales, and, in the time he or she puts in, keeps knocking it out of the park, you might decide not to care about how many actual hours he or she is working.

Or you may decide that this is exactly what brought you to entrepreneurship in the first place: to get away from the cold-hearted, evil world of big business that doesn't care about individuals. And that it is okay to allow a partner who is distracted to continue to take his or her full share because the situation is not his or her fault and not related to the business.

Another common challenge arises when one partner ends up with the ability to effectively control a significant part of the business. As a result, that partner has actual leverage over the other. You could be on either side of that.

If you are on the "better" side and are stronger in the business, consider that there may be times down the road when the roles flip, so don't necessarily rush to insist on changes in your financial or management arrangement. If you don't seek a change, a good partner will appreciate it and maybe even become more committed to the business.

If you are on the "worse" side, consider at least offering to adjust the arrangement, especially if you perceive a real risk that the other partner may try to leave without you. If you do offer to alter things, something flexible may make sense where you leave open the possibility of readjusting if the situation changes down the road.

But beware of arrangements that are designed for constant adjustment, or that leave you almost competing with your partner to "earn" the better deal. If that is the case, make sure there are enough incentives built in to help each other and benefit from each other's success. Or be in an arrangement where your incentives are based on things that do not overlap or going after non-competing business opportunities.

One option in this situation is to take a look at whether a partition of the business is possible. Are you in a service business where one of you has a certain amount of client business and the other has a lot more? Could you amicably part, each taking your own clients if you are unable to agree on some sort of adjustment? This happens all the time in the law business.

And what to do with the partner who is doing what a salaried employee could easily do? This is a tougher one, since you made the deal you did knowing the partner's capabilities and limitations. If you did not negotiate an ability to buy out the partner up-front, and you want to stop continuing to pay a windfall to him or her, consider offering a buyout, if you are able.

Or again, decide that it is right to stick to your commitment. You knew going in that this could mean big bucks for your new partner if things worked out. Neither decision is right or wrong. Even if you offer to buy out your partner, you are not mandating it. If you have a deal that permits a buyout, you should not feel bad if you choose to exercise it, since everyone knew going in that was a possibility.

Sadly, when things become more challenging with a partner, whether because of a change in the business or a change in the partner's circumstances, you often see the partner's true colors for the first time. Things he or she has been dying to say for years, not necessarily positive, suddenly come out. Try your best to take this in stride. Stress sometimes causes people to say things they don't mean.

Then again, stress can give people strength to say things they have been meaning to say for a long time. If you sense that is the case, do your best to use the moment to try to air and deal with whatever issues you have both been hesitating to discuss previously.

Personality Traits Yielding Burnout or Loss of Focus

Who is more likely to forget our whole "marathon" metaphor and burn themselves out? Who is more likely to yield to a new idea and take their energies away from their base? In both cases I have seen way too many businesses fail because of an entrepreneur's inability to sense the warning signs to avoid these dreaded mistakes.

The most likely to burn out are those feeling like they have the most to prove because of an intense fear of failure, the workaholic or work hard/play hard types, and the micromanagers who forget to see the forest for the trees.

A healthy fear of failure is okay and can be a real motivator. If, however, you came to entrepreneurship overwhelmingly afraid to fail, that could lead to devoting way more energy to building the business than you are capable of. You don't apply any of the techniques we have described to pace yourself or give yourself a break, both physically and mentally. You are up very late dealing with everything and you suddenly find yourself simply exhausted.

The workaholic type also can easily burn out, as can those who work hard and play hard. If you do nothing but deal with the business 24/7, or spend all your free time partying, there can easily hit a moment where you simply shut down.

Last, someone who has an overwhelming need to involve him or herself in every tiny detail and facet of the business also can wipe out. You find yourself reviewing the actions of underlings at 3 AM even though they have shown themselves over and over to be capable, and to provide useful and thorough reports to you of their activities.

In truth, while there is much advice to give to these folks, as described in these pages, they are simply less likely to take it because you are talking about aspects of their personality that are difficult to change. This is why Chapter 2 suggests that if you do not have many of the traits which are more likely to lead to entrepreneurial success, you may not want to even consider it in the first place.

But this does not stop many, even though they don't quite fit the mold! In all cases, again, a business coach can help you work on some of these challenges to try to get yourself away from your default setting that works negatively in this circumstance.

In addition, having a strong partner whom you can really trust is sometimes a way to ameliorate the effects of a personality that could lead to burnout. If you really believe in the person you are in the business with, this might help to reduce your concerns about failure, working too hard, or managing every detail.

Moving on to individuals with the unique personalities most likely to lose focus when a new idea comes, I think you can see this challenge in someone who is too much of a dreamer, someone more likely to be bored as the business grows, or someone maybe with a little bit of attention deficit disorder or something similar.

We did talk about the importance of the big dream as part of being ready to be a successful entrepreneur. For some, the whole entrepreneurial thing is all about the dream—the excitement of something new. They love to tinker, and to write down ideas and thoughts. Whenever they see a product or service, they think, "Can I do that better?"

If it is almost entirely about that, you may find yourself not succeeding. If your focus is easily pulled away because the details of running a business or even acting as strategic coordinator and cheerleader are just not your thing, the exciting business you started simply may not get off the ground properly.

The classic example, of course, in the life sciences area, is a talented scientist who develops a real potential breakthrough. She believes she can build a business around it, but frankly has never done so. But her big dreams led to this moment, and she wants to ride it as far as she can. Almost immediately, however, the details of starting, building, and running a business are clearly not for her.

She does the best she can, and somehow manages to raise some money and add a few employees, but while she continues to believe in her development, is just much happier in her lab than in her company office. Sure enough, something else comes along in the lab that excites her. What to do?

In our scientist's case, she needs to admit to herself that entrepreneurship probably is not really for her. She should consider either licensing her developments to existing companies, or bringing in professional managers to run the businesses she creates. Her focus is and should remain on the next big development.

As we have covered, if you are more likely to be bored when the business grows, even if you have strong business abilities, the new idea is more likely to distract you. Here again, think about various options such as a sale of the first business or handing it over. Or work to train yourself to stay focused on the first project until it reaches a natural transition point, instead of an unnatural one based on your loss of focus.

Last, do you have ADD, ADHD, or another medical issue concerning your attention or focus? This is nothing to be ashamed of; it is quite common among the U.S. population. It is also unusually prevalent among entrepreneurs.

Why that is, one can conjecture. Maybe these folks have a tougher time fitting into a more traditional work situation. According to WebMD.com, "Adults with ADHD may have difficulty with time management, organizational skills, goal setting, and employment. They may also have problems with relationships, self-esteem, and addictions." Some also think they are more likely to have an intense, creative side.

I once represented a small company being sold to a larger entrepreneurial venture. The buyer was a company run by a very well-known young man. He had dropped out of college, and started and built the company, in the software business, very rapidly. Let's call him Mick, because he had become a bit of a rock star in his world. Mick was indeed known as an incredible programmer.

My clients and I went to the buyer's offices for a meeting to finalize the last negotiating points between the parties. Mick clearly had trouble paying attention and sitting still. This actually worked a bit to his advantage, as my clients were clearly concerned about upsetting him or worrying him. They were anxious to complete the deal with such a well-known player.

At one point we reached a bit of an impasse on a fairly major issue relating to when and how the purchase price would be paid to my clients. Mick dramatically sat up, pushed his chair back, and announced to the group, "Time to take my Ritalin!"

He pulled out a pill bottle, took out a pill and downed it with a swig of water. He then walked out. As we know, Ritalin is a common treatment for

ADD and ADHD. It is also sometimes abused by college students to help their focus during studying.

My associate and I looked at each other after Mick left the room. Mick's lawyer, who was also sitting there, gave us kind of a blank stare. We assumed he had seen this before. The lawyer asked if we needed a little time. He left.

My clients, frankly, had little leverage in the situation. Their credit line was used up, their family's and friends' money pretty much ran out, and no new financing sources seemed available. And while their revenues and the cachet of their product were slowly growing, the overhead needed was simply tapping all of that and more.

A sale made the most sense and was their only chance other than shutting down. The two founders would be employed by Mick to oversee a division selling their products. Mick's company's overhead would absorb the revenues and hopefully make it profitable. After about 15 minutes' discussion, my clients decided to give in on the point rather than risk Mick never coming back into the room. They understood it might have been simply a tactic and Mick might ultimately back down. He had made clear that he loved the product my clients had built, which fit very nicely into the image Mick had created for himself and his company.

Sure enough, we closed the sale. My clients unfortunately were let go after a year, but actually started a new similar but non-competitive business. Amazingly, though, with his marketing muscle Mick took my clients' product and shot it up to one of the top brands around.

I have read in recent years that Mick's business was in trouble. It is private, so no one really knows. About three years ago he was forced to make a number of moves to keep his business going, including selling off divisions and putting off expansion plans. The rumors were that he was deep in debt. Loss of focus? Maybe.

Uncle Lenny

Meet my uncle Leonard Rivkin. Lenny, now in his late 80s but not fully retired, built what is still the largest law firm on Long Island, New York, with about 150 lawyers. Lenny is about as close to someone doing everything right in building a business as I have personally witnessed.

Let's go through his fascinating story a bit as a fitting coda to this writing. Much more detail is available in Lenny's terrific autobiography, called *May It Please the Court*, published in 2000. Before I went to the New York major law firms, my first job out of law school was with his firm, now known as Rivkin Radler.

Lenny grew up in Far Rockaway, New York, the son of a local physician. (My mother is his sister.) After his first year of college at the University of Virginia, he joined the Army and fought valiantly in World War II. For his bravery during the Battle of the Bulge he was awarded the coveted Silver Star and a purple heart. Indeed he is the very definition of the "Greatest Generation."

Thanks to the GI Bill, after the war Lenny was able to return to the University of Virginia and complete college and law school in just three years. When he graduated, he assumed a decent job would be available in New York City when he returned home. After all, he was both a top scholar and a war hero. Sadly, at the time (the early 1950s), he was not able to find a job in Manhattan. Lenny returned home to Far Rockaway quite dejected to say the least.

With my grandparents' help, Lenny decided to give a shot to opening up his own one-man law practice. He rented a room in the back of an insurance agent's office in Freeport, Long Island. Every Tuesday night he made his way to the local bar association meetings, where lawyers got together and talked about cases. Finally one guy had a conflict and asked him to handle a small personal injury, "slip and fall" case. Lenny won!

Then came a few more cases. Then he beat the insurance companies that provide payment for injuries a bunch more times. He even landed a big case involving a major spill on Staten Island that got some media attention. He got paid only if his client won, but if he did then he would get a percentage of the recovery.

He did so well that the insurance companies finally convinced him to switch sides and start representing them in defending these cases. They handed him tons of small cases, leading to more lawyers and growth. When I interned there in high school in the late 1970s there were already about 35 lawyers, including one then-brand-new lawyer who these days, decades later, is managing partner of the firm.

Len ended up working for a number of years on issues surrounding the failure of a national bank located on Long Island, leading again to lots of press. There is no question that Lenny's skills as a trial lawyer were unsurpassed. He was tough, but he knew when it was time to settle. Much like the larger than life fictional TV lawyer Denny Crane, played by William Shatner on *Boston Legal*, many local attorneys literally shuddered when they learned that the great Leonard Rivkin was coming to court personally against them.

Then came the big kahuna of cases when he was asked to represent Dow Chemical Co. in the so-called "Agent Orange" case. The U.S. government used a chemical called Agent Orange as a defoliant during the Vietnam War to clear forest areas, revealing enemy locations. Dozens of manufacturers were required to produce the chemical based on government specifications.

Unfortunately, it appeared that the defoliant may have caused some serious illnesses in many soldiers.

The case went on for a number of years and was simply huge, not to mention covered extensively in the press, and Len led the charge on Dow's behalf, but together with a number of other chemical manufacturers.

Many, including their fellow veteran Len Rivkin, felt terrible for the soldiers. But the claimants had a legal problem, because they were going to have some difficulty proving the connection of Agent Orange to their illnesses, which might have come from other causes. The link of causation, key to a personal injury case, was somewhat weak.

Another major problem in the case was the so-called "government contractor" defense, where a manufacturer says, "Hey, I was required to make this stuff in wartime and to do so exactly as the government directed me, so I can't be responsible." And unfortunately, for various reasons, soldiers in this situation cannot sue the military or U.S. government.

In the end, Lenny negotiated a settlement of less than $200 million from all the manufacturers, which was put in a trust to divide among the claimants. The ill veterans each got some money, even though the manufacturers felt they could have prevailed ultimately. It was, however, politically a smart thing to do. In the end it was considered a huge victory for Dow and the other chemical companies, and of course for Len Rivkin and his firm.

After the Dow case in the early 1980s, Lenny became a real superstar in legal circles throughout the country—getting awards, speaking everywhere, receiving honorary degrees, you name it. And the firm continued to grow, at one point having offices in about five different cities. Now back to its roots on Long Island, it is still one of the leading firms doing major national environmental law cases and, as I mentioned, is still the largest firm on Long Island.

But not everything went perfectly as the firm grew. There were a handful of name changes as the firm brought in successful senior partners who either did not live up to their promise or whose egos did not permit them to share the spotlight easily. Len and the team eventually learned: stick with one brand. For the last 25 years or so it has been simply Rivkin Radler.

The firm also faced challenges with its expansion into other cities. They were dependent on partners and clients who were not necessarily long-term in their outlook. The overhead was having an impact as Len realized that much of the work could be handled from their main Long Island office. So eventually everything was consolidated back to where it all started. Len realized that expansion for its own sake is not always in a company's best interest.

While I'm sure you enjoyed that homage to a great man, it's important context to my review of Len's entrepreneurial chops. He is indeed a natural leader, overseeing the operations of his firm as it grew successfully and profitably. His stature and personality were outsized, yet his ego was right-sized. The ways literally parted in the firm's hallways when he was passing through. He was, and is, respected throughout the firm.

Lenny is also a true macromanager. One of his favorite remarks to junior partners was "Don't bother me with the mishigas." (While the real Yiddish definition is "craziness," he meant it to refer to the small stuff.)

He was always looking ahead and planning for growth optimistically but cautiously. For example, right after the Dow case things were really hopping. The firm decided to take multiple floors in a new building going up. Instead of just laying out the money for the move, or borrowing it expensively from a bank, he arranged an industrial revenue bond from the county he was in. By borrowing from the county, he got much more favorable terms, a very low interest rate, and a longer term payout. The firm still occupies that space today following a beautiful recent top to bottom renovation.

Len did not hesitate to use the "D" word and delegate. He had many underlings both in managing the firm and servicing clients who were given a significant amount of responsibility. But he kept an eye on things. I remember one meeting during the one year I was an attorney there in which Len met with the team of 10 lawyers of which I was a part. He had clearly done his homework. He pointed to one guy and said, "Your letters are too tough and strong." To another, "Your correspondence is too weak." Trust, but verify.

Work/less work balance was indeed the order of the day for Len during his working years. He always took good amounts of time off, even if it meant taking work with him. There is no question he worked very hard. The family still kids him about having one of the very first car phones back in the 1970s. (You had to call the marine operator to make a call.)

But Lenny knew how important family and personal time was. His passions were fishing and boating. They gave him perspective and an ability to recharge. And family is very important to Len. Nothing is better for him than sitting down on the couch to watch football with everyone after a wonderful Thanksgiving dinner.

Len never really faced burnout as he carefully paced himself. I think that when he retired it was more out of boredom. The firm was very busy with many cases, but he had brought in some great folks who were handling things without much need for his involvement. He trained them too well! He had also remarried a wonderful lady following the untimely death of my aunt, and of course wanted to enjoy life with his new wife.

In addition, I think Len enjoyed life at his firm less once it became rather large and bureaucratic. In my early years after starting my own firm, he told me that part of him wished for the simplicity of the days when everyone in the firm could fit around one conference table.

But I know he was proud of the firm he created and grew. I remember when he brought his then-elderly mother (my grandmother, may she rest in peace) to tour the new office built with the revenue bonds. There was a beautiful partners' dining room, massive conference rooms, three full floors of offices, and of course a gorgeous and very large office for Len with a view of Manhattan. He was beaming with pride, as was my grandmother.

A funny story I remember from my time there is telling. Early on Len had decided that another partner should run the firm on a day-to-day basis as managing partner, reporting to him as senior partner. The managing partner at the time sent a memo to all in the office, saying that the firm had now grown so much that people should no longer send memos to or from someone using just their initials. Please use full names from now on read the edict. Obviously this was before e-mail.

The very next day came a memo to all in the firm about something unrelated. It was written as from LLR (Lenny's initials), clearly flouting the prior directive from his managing partner. So either Lenny read the memo and was making a point, or didn't read it because he was in fact, frankly above it. But you can bet his wonderful longtime secretary, who typed the memo, had read the previous memo from the managing partner. She knew that no one would question Len continuing to use his initials. In writing this book I embarked on an investigation of initials-gate and determined that Len has absolutely no recollection of the incident.

Until his retirement, I think Len enjoyed working on cases and helping the firm's image through what seemed to be endless accolades coming his way. But he addressed his boredom in one of the ways we describe here: by handing the reins to others and moving on. He moved to Florida, and a mere 20 years later decided he had "flunked retirement," and moved back to Long Island, where he visits his office regularly and spends time with his family.

So thanks, Len, for being a great mentor and friend, for being an inspiration to so many, and for building a true institution the right way—by letting it grow beyond just your imprint so that it can continue for generations to come. Who knows—maybe Len's granddaughter, in law school as of this writing, could end up there one day to join his son, now a senior partner. And thanks for letting my readers learn from your success.

Therefore . . .

In the end, some and maybe even most of the traps and challenges described in this book are unavoidable when considering starting a new business. But this does not mean they are insurmountable. Gauging your proclivities will help you determine whether the decision to become an entrepreneur is right for you, and evaluating the potential problems associated with starting your own business is an invaluable step in the process.

I think most entrepreneurs believe that dealing with all the challenges and laments in their way is almost always worth it in order to have the freedom to pursue business opportunities unfettered by infrastructure, bosses, and in many cases even partners.

It's as much about the joy of that freedom as it is about the ambition for financial success. I have many regrets, in the sense that there are certainly things I would have done differently in my various entrepreneurial endeavors. But I have no regret about choosing the path I did, and I think almost all entrepreneurs will tell you the same, gray hair notwithstanding.

So get to it!

About the Author

David N. Feldman, a corporate and securities attorney, is a senior partner of Richardson & Patel LLP in New York. Feldman received a bachelor of science in economics from the Wharton School of Business at the University of Pennsylvania in 1982 and his Juris Doctor in 1985 from the University of Pennsylvania Law School. Feldman is the former chairman of Wharton's worldwide Alumni Association Board. He is also a frequent public speaker, seminar leader, and counsel on issues unique to small and microcap companies, and is an active advocate with regulators and Congress on small business issues. His clients include public and private companies, investment banks, venture capital firms, and high net worth individuals. His blog at www.DavidFeldmanBlog.com is visited by thousands each month and has been named a LexisNexis top 25 corporate law blog. Feldman has appeared on Bloomberg TV and National Public Radio, and been quoted in the *New York Times, Wall Street Journal, Financial Times, New York Law Journal, The Deal, Forbes, Entrepreneur, CFO* magazine, and others. David is the author of *Reverse Mergers* (Bloomberg Press, 2006 and second edition, 2009), which TheStreet.com has called the "seminal text" on reverse mergers. He is also a contributor to *An Issuer's Guide to PIPEs* (Bloomberg Press, 2009) and *PIPES: A Guide to Private Investments in Public Equity, Revised and Updated Edition* (Bloomberg Press, 2005).

Index